MW00667101

# SURVIVING
# *life*

Lydia,
2 Cor. 1:4
Bless You
Scott + Sandy

# SURVIVING *life*

*one family's fight to survive*
*& the discoveries that saved them*

Scott Tremp MC & Sandy Tremp IAC-CC

Tate Publishing & *Enterprises*

Published by Tate Publishing & Enterprises, LLC
127 E. Trade Center Terrace | Mustang, Oklahoma 73064 USA
1.888.361.9473 | www.tatepublishing.com

Tate Publishing is committed to excellence in the publishing industry. The company reflects the philosophy established by the founders, based on Psalm 68:11,
*"The Lord gave the word and great was the company of those who published it."*


*Cover design by Kellie Southerland*
*Author photo by Mimi Jae Photography, Julie A. Jacobson*
*Interior design by Stefanie Rane*

Published in the United States of America

ISBN: 978-1-61739-252-8
1. Self-Help, Personal Growth, General
2. Biography & Autobiography, Personal Memoirs
10.07.30

# DEDICATION

To our sons, who endured much through this difficult journey.

# ACKNOWLEDGMENTS

The help of many wonderful people has gone into our recovery process. Our undying gratitude extends to each and every one of you. Toby, Judy N., Judy G., Karen, Rene, Howard, Susan, Ruth, and Lori: were it not for your input and influence, we would not be the people we are today. Thank you!

We would like to thank our families for their prayers and support as we traveled this difficult journey, especially Mom and Dad, Kris, Theresa, Bob, Deb, Steve, and Deena. Without your selfless sacrifices, much of the help we received would not have been possible. Your enduring love and faithful support carried us through our darkest of hours. We love you!

To our Core Group: Commander Bill and Kathy Campbell, Steven and Andrean Cunningham, Christel Snodgrass, Terry Kohuth, and Kathy Garrett. Thank you for encouraging us to give our very best. When we thought we'd laid it all on the table, you insisted we had more. Your belief in us, in our story, and in our "survival skills" gave us the encouragement to push through. You guys are the greatest!

Ashley, our editor, your wisdom and insights helped us tighten this work and make it better than we could have imagined. Thank you!

How could we forget those additional few who encouraged, uplifted, and inspired us? Thank you to Bob and Linda Galloway, Lori Briesacher, John and Rhonda Wincek, Mabel Sawyer, Dr. Mark Heiser, Bill and Trish Carroll, Joni and Steve, and, of course, our sons, who patiently supported our writing process and offered helpful suggestions along the way.

# TABLE OF CONTENTS

# *Introduction: What You Need To Know Before Reading This Book*

As individuals who've had our fair share of life-changing crises, we desire to share our journey and the insights we discovered along the way. In so doing, we have created what we trust is a unique blend of our family's compelling struggle to survive and a life-changing, easy to follow self-help book.

Through a transparent vulnerability, we walk our readers through our pain, heartache, setbacks, failures, and victories. We then coach you, step by step, through five simple yet powerful life skills based on biblical principles that will help you rise above your own adversity.

Whether you are a self-help junkie or simply enjoy a good read, it is our prayer that this book will profoundly impact your life.

To assist you as you read, it is important to understand the following:

- Throughout the text, we each take turns speaking and at times speak as one voice. To help you navigate these sections, we have designated the beginning of these paragraphs with our names.
- For the continuity of our story and ultimately the application of the life lessons, our account demands that we share uncomfortable facts. However, we have worked diligently to protect the personal rights of all involved, for it is neither our desire nor our intent to identify any individuals or cause them harm or distress. Therefore, we use fictitious names for every individual and organization involved, with the exception of ourselves.
- The trusted family member whose actions traumatized and disrupted our lives is referred to as Cat, short for Catalyst. Though we'd never choose to repeat these horrific experiences, we are grateful for the powerful changes our suffering ultimately brought about. God used these trials as catalysts to grow and develop us and ultimately draw us closer to him.

# *Without Warning*

Thanksgiving is a time most families anticipate long-awaited reunions with loved ones. However, less than a week before this celebration of togetherness, our world was plunged into darkness and despair.

## FRIDAY, NOVEMBER 22, 1991

SCOTT

I had just wrapped up a long day of painting, an interim career I was finding quite unsatisfying. Today's project had been the exterior of an industrial building. After meeting up with Sandy and our three young sons, our family was finally headed home in our respective vehicles. As we caravanned through the city streets, I wondered what might be awaiting me at home. Would I be able to relax this evening, or would I spend my downtime getting the boys to help me clean the house? Sandy was unable to hold down employment and even struggled to keep up with the household responsibilities lately. No matter how much I helped, she was often not able to maintain the stamina or energy to get through a day. Her health issues were one reason I resigned as the pastor of a growing, independent Bible church and moved to Arizona, where her large, close-knit extended family lived. This move meant leaving my home state of Michigan and, sadly, my family. We hoped that the bright sunshine and the absence of ministry stresses would allow Sandy the opportunity to recuperate and regain her former vitality.

Little did I know of the tempest that raged within my wife on this day. If I had known, could I have done something to avert the destruction of that fateful storm? I guess I'll never know.

I lazily awoke from a pre-dinner nap, the grumbling in my stomach reminding me just how hungry I was. Curious about dinner, I ventured into the kitchen. The scene that confronted me as I rounded the corner still haunts me to this very day. There on the floor, pressed up tightly against the cupboards as though trying to disappear from life itself, was the woman I loved, curled into a fetal position.

I rushed over to Sandy, my feet barely touching the floor. Stunned, shocked, and confused at her condition, I hastily dropped to my wife's side. "Honey, what's wrong?" I cried out, wanting to hold her but not sure what to do, given the surreal state she was in. Words could not express my bewilderment as I struggled to grasp what was happening.

I was at a loss for what to do. As my fear and frustration mounted, I noticed Sandy's hands had a stranglehold on her hair. I reached out to disentangle her fingers from her short locks, but at my touch she quickly recoiled and began rocking herself. I was afraid to touch her again, worried as to how she might react a second time. Taking great care not to touch her skin, I gently brushed her warm chestnut hair from her face and looked intently into her blue-green eyes, hoping to find some answer there. All that returned to me was a vacant stare. Her absent gaze and her methodical rocking shook me to my very core.

Fighting to reach her, I cried out, "Sandy, sweetheart, can you hear me? Honey, you're scaring me! What's wrong?" *Is she unconscious? Is she hurt? Is she bleeding?* I couldn't find any external signs of trauma. She was obviously still breathing. My mind raced as I desperately sought to identify the problem. No matter what I did, I got no response beyond the incessant rocking. It was as though Sandy had left me and gone somewhere I could not follow. Only an empty shell remained.

Our three sons—ages eight, seven, and five—were contentedly playing with their GI Joes in the family room when they overheard my frightened pleas for Sandy to respond. Quickly abandoning their imaginary skirmish, they hurried into the kitchen. I couldn't let them see her like this. I could only imagine what seeing their mother in this state would do to them.

"It's okay, boys," I struggled to reassure them while discreetly blocking their view. "Mommy just fell down; she'll be okay. Go in the living room and watch TV." Picking up on the intensity of my voice, they quickly turned and made their way to the television.

After many desperate and unsuccessful attempts to get Sandy to respond, I accepted the fact that something was terribly wrong—something beyond my ability to fix. I needed to get help. Carefully lifting her, I carried her to our bed, where I hoped she'd be more comfortable, while I figured out what to do next. After reassuring the boys, I placed a call to Bill, her counselor, whom she'd been seeing to help her manage her stress; I figured he was the best place to start.

I quickly filled him in on the details, and he agreed that I should bring her to his office immediately. Unable to find anyone to watch the boys on such short notice, I secured them in the car, tossing in a bag of toys and a box of crackers I'd grabbed as we ran out the door. I gently lifted Sandy, carried her to the car, and rushed us all to Bill's office. As I drove, I prayed frantically, begging God for help.

Keeping my focus on the road proved difficult. I continued talking to Sandy, hoping she would eventually respond to my voice. My concern for my wife trumped all else.

The boys realized that something was very wrong and began to pepper me with questions about their mommy. I was desperate to control my own fear, calm theirs, and connect with Sandy.

The inside of the car was nearly in a state of chaos as the cumulative fear swelled. Suddenly, despite the cries coming from the back seat, I heard a whisper coming from Sandy's direction. There it was again. She had mumbled something! Overjoyed that I had broken through and made some sort of connection, I nearly drove off the road as I leaned toward her, straining to listen, willing her to talk.

"Honey, I'm here. Sweetheart, what's wrong? Are you okay?"

There it was again. What was she saying? Then finally I was able to make it out: "I'll be a good girl, I promise. I'll be a good girl."

*Oh God, what is going on? Why would she be saying this? What's happened to my wife? None of this makes any sense.* Had my brief slumber only an hour before turned into a nightmare from which I was unable to wake? Questioning my reality, I pinched myself. The sharp pain confirmed that this was no dream.

"It's okay, honey; you're okay. I'm right here," I continued, attempting to comfort myself as much as my wife, but her bizarre mumbling persisted. My heart winced at each repeat of the disturbingly pitiful phrase.

I pulled into the parking lot as quickly as possible in my desperate rush for help. Hurrying the boys out, I ran to Sandy's door. As I reached to pick her up, her body stiffened at my touch. *What is going on? She has never responded to me like this before.*

Fear chased me, bearing down on my heart, as I rushed her into Bill's office with three frightened children at my heels. Meeting us at the door, Bill guided us back to his office. I could see that his concern matched mine the moment he laid eyes on her. We laid Sandy on his couch, where he immediately began to check her vital signs. I found it strange that a counselor would have the training and equipment to test one's vitals, but I was thankful he did. I took the boys back into the outer room and attempted to distract them with the toys and the meager meal of crackers and water.

Several minutes later, Bill called me back into his office, where Sandy remained in her catatonic stupor. He too had been unable to connect with her. Bill believed she had experienced some sort of mental break and insisted I get her to a psychiatric hospital as soon as possible.

My knowledge of such hospitals was minimal at best. I had no idea where to take her, so Bill made a few suggestions. I decided my best course of action would be to go back home and develop a game plan since Sandy's vital signs were okay and she didn't seem to be in any immediate danger.

When we returned home, I was unable to get Sandy to eat, so I got her settled into bed. Clearly not herself, she was very frightened and withdrawn, more like a child than the adult I knew and loved. Although I was pursuing my post-graduate degree in counseling, I had little knowledge of a problem of this magnitude.

In the dining room, the boys finished up their drive-thru-burgers and appeared more than ready for bed. It was obvious that they were worried about their mother, but the special dinner treat I'd picked up on the way home seemed to temporarily abate their fears.

After settling the boys into bed and reassuring them that Mommy would soon be okay, I checked on Sandy. Thanks to her previously prescribed medication, she was sound asleep. I was grateful that she slept peacefully, for I knew there would be little sleep for me this night.

I took advantage of the quiet to call Sandy's family, my family, and friends to inform them of our situation and ask for much-needed prayer. They were all obviously concerned and asked that I keep them up-to-date on her progress.

Once I finally fell into bed, I tossed and turned. Between my periodic checks on Sandy and my racing mind, sleep simply would not come. I struggled to grasp and process all that had happened. There were many lingering questions that demanded answers. I had no solutions, but that didn't stop my mind from struggling to figure things out. I obsessed about things I would need to do and worried about Sandy. Praying, I asked God for help, direction, healing for my wife, and sleep for me.

At the first sign of light I stumbled out of bed and with a renewed purpose began making plans. Being a list maker, I wrote down and then prioritized the steps I would take. I included the hospitals I would call and the questions I would ask. I was a man on a mission. I was determined to find a hospital where Sandy could get the best help possible.

As the boys sleepily emerged from their room, I reluctantly set my agenda aside. Spending time with them over breakfast, I encouraged them to talk about what they were feeling. I was concerned about how they were handling the situation. Again, I reassured them Mommy would be okay. Eager to watch their Saturday morning cartoons, they soon abandoned their empty cereal bowls and headed for the TV. With them happily occupied, I checked on Sandy and was comforted to find her still sound asleep. I was thankful that for this moment all was calm.

Optimistic and hopeful, I sent up a quick prayer for guidance and began making my calls, the first of which was to our health insurance agent. Expecting to find hospital options, I was shocked instead to discover that our policy did not include mental health benefits. The momentum with which my day began suddenly ground to a screeching halt. Sensing my disappointment, my agent sympathized and suggested I call various hospitals to see if any would work with me on a cash basis. One option was a publicly funded facility. It was more closely suited to our budget, but I believed Sandy needed more specialized care than I felt they would offer.

Re-gathering my stalled momentum, I decided not to let money be an issue and began calling the hospitals on my list, both in- and out-of-state. After hours of being put on hold and asking and answering a myriad of questions, I finally settled on a facility that seemed to be the best fit for Sandy. It was a reputable hospital with a Christian wing staffed with Christian professionals. With that settled, I now faced the daunting task of funding such a decision. This particular hospital required payment in advance. Financially, we were in decent shape, but we did not have the extra money required to cover the high cost of hospitalization. Unable to resolve the financial conundrum, I decided to call my family for advice and wisdom.

As they answered the phone, I skipped the normal pleasantries and got right to the point. I shared the information I had gathered from a number of facilities and told them I had narrowed my options to one in particular that I felt would provide Sandy with the best care. I also let them know that our insurance would not cover any of the $6,000 a week the hospital charged and that a full week's payment was required in advance. Before I could get their thoughts, they offered me their credit card number and encouraged me to get her in immediately. Expressing deep concern for Sandy, they shared their regrets about not living closer and their inability to be of more help. I thanked them profusely, knowing this was a very real sacrifice for them. I assured them that their generosity was more than helpful and their love and concern were comforting. Disconnecting their call, I immediately phoned the hospital and made the necessary arrangements.

Dropping the boys off with Tom and Brenda, a couple of Sandy's relatives who were glad to help, I rushed Sandy to the hospital. My hopes were lifted; my wife was finally going to get the help she desperately needed!

After the lengthy process of checking Sandy in, she was whisked away for an even longer examination. As I anxiously awaited the report from the doctor, my mind struggled, fighting to make sense of the surreal circumstances in which we suddenly found ourselves. Any attempts to understand were met with confusion. The more my confusion grew, the deeper the razor-sharp talons of anxiety and fear dug into my emotional flesh. It was becoming increasingly difficult to sit, so I began pacing the room. My tensions were interrupted when the doctor finally entered.

"Mr. Tremp, hello, I'm Dr. Morrison. I'll be Sandy's psychiatrist. Why don't we have a seat?" The big man smiled as he extended his hand with genuine warmth that was both disarming and calming. I was relieved that Sandy would have such a caring and gentle doctor with whom to work.

"We have just spent the last few hours examining and evaluating Sandy. She is in a very delicate place, as you well know," the doctor said.

As he continued to explain Sandy's condition, my anxiety mounted, making it difficult to concentrate, let alone comprehend his psychological jargon. The doctor's words jumbled in my mind. Desperate for him to get to the point, I boldly interrupted, "Doctor, is she going to be okay? When can I take her home?"

"Scott"—he paused, as if to soften the blow—"you need to prepare yourself, because Sandy might never be the same again." His words slammed into me with the force of a freight train. I was glad I was sitting down because if I wasn't, I think I would have fallen over.

"She's had a severe mental break," he continued. "In cases like this, we recommend at least six months of hospitalization to begin with. Then we will evaluate where to go from there. She has a long and tough road ahead of her."

"But will she eventually be okay?" I pleaded.

"I can't make any guarantees at this point; it's too early to tell," Dr. Morrison said.

I was not prepared to handle this news. I needed hope, but instead, an incredible sense of hopelessness began to settle deep within my being. This desperation would claim its place in my heart for some time to come.

# *The Perfect Storm*

SANDY

Chronic fatigue plagued my life. The exhausting condition hit me in 1987, at the age of twenty-four, nearly a year after the birth of our third son. Between the CFS (chronic fatigue syndrome) and a thyroid problem I did not yet understand, I often lacked the energy it took to keep up with life in general, let alone the responsibilities of running a household of five. At the time, there was little understanding of CFS and its debilitating effects. As a result, neither Scott nor I truly understood the impact these conditions had on my daily life. I would often push myself until I would literally crash and burn. Only then would it dawn on us that I had certain limitations. On those days when I felt semi-okay, I would carelessly forget my physical state and then not understand why I couldn't keep up with everyone else. At these times I often berated myself unmercifully for what I, and what I assumed others, interpreted as laziness. Though we didn't understand it at the time, my forgetfulness, or rather, my distancing myself from my problems, was actually a coping mechanism. We would soon discover that I developed this ability as a small child as a means of protecting myself from the terrible abuse I had experienced and subsequently repressed.

As a result of my health, my home was in a constant state of disarray. Devoid of the vitality and drive to accomplish much, I was feeling less and less competent in my abilities in general in addition to my responsibilities as a homemaker. The energy I did have, I lavishly poured first into my husband, then my sons, and then other relationships, but not my domestic duties. Scott and the boys might not have lived in the cleanest of homes, but they knew I was always available and that my love for them ran deep. However, placing my relationships ahead of all else came at a steep price. Because I was such a pleaser, my choice to put others first left me with not only an untidy home but with the deep, hidden ache of personal failure.

Loving people was a double-edged sword. I longed for the connection it brought while I agonized over the feelings of inadequacy it stirred. Living for others, I strived to bring happiness to those around me. Yet, no matter how hard I tried to please, I always felt I failed in one way or another. Even when those around me were happy, I still found myself continually scanning faces and body language alike, my antenna sharply tuned to pick up any disappointment or frustration.

The weariness of my physical state merged with the overwhelming condemnation in my inner world. These then collided with the disappointments I personalized from others, creating ideal conditions for the storm that was brewing on that fateful November day. Initiated by a hidden, long-forgotten past, complicated by my own confusion and self-abasement, seeded by whispered lies, it was perfect makings for the perfect storm.

## FRIDAY, NOVEMBER 22, 1991

The day began like most of my days: I woke to the call of the alarm long before my body, still exhausted after a full night's sleep, was willing to move. Smelling the delicious aroma of the coffee Scott had brewed, I longed for the benefit of that same pick-me-up. I was not afforded such luxury, as just a few sips of the dark tonic set my nerves on edge, giving me the jitters and only exhausting me further. Instead, I prayed for the grace and energy to make it through another day. Had I known what lurked on the horizon, I might have given a little more consideration to that simple prayer.

Handing them their freshly packed lunches, I kissed our two older sons, sending them off for the short walk to school. They were in the second and first grade. Before they made it over the threshold, I embraced each of them in one last hug I simply couldn't resist. Scott had long since left for work, kissing me good-bye even before I was fully awake. Having transitioned from crew foreman to owning his own painting business a year before, his days started early, while it was still dark. He was a great provider, a man who loved and sacrificed daily for his family. He was, and remains to this day, the love of my life.

Soon our youngest and I were out the door for the short trip to the Christian kindergarten he attended. Leaving him with his teacher after an equal slathering of love and affection, I rushed off to the hospital to capture a few moments with my grandmother. The doctors feared she was nearing her final days. Although my day was already full of commitments and demands, I decided a short visit with Grandma could not hurt. The realization that my time with her was coming to an end heightened my desire to be with her every moment I could. The regret of my busy schedule settled over me like a dark heavy cloud. I struggled to maintain control. The last thing I needed to do was walk into Grandma's room a blubbering mess. Hoping to change my mood, I shifted my thoughts to the hectic day before me, which probably was not the greatest idea. There was a sinister storm brewing, and that simple act of considering my hectic day afforded it just the opening it needed. Though still in the distance, its icy winds began mocking me for my over-commitment, laughing maniacally at my inflated sense of self-importance.

Shaking off the sudden chill brought on by these disturbing thoughts, I made my way into the room. Grandma and I reminisced, taking pleasure in fond memories we shared while I lovingly stroked her frail hand. She assured me of her readiness to meet her heavenly Father, encouraging me far more than I could possibly hope to encourage her, though I tried. At her request, I softly sang a few of her favorite hymns while she closed her eyes and basked in the love I knew she felt. As I sang, I caught a glimpse of the clock hanging on her wall. A surge of nerves passed through me, an errant bolt of lightning striking from the impending clouds. My voice squeaked and I nearly jolted out of my seat. I had spent more time with Grandma than my schedule allowed. The day had just begun and I was already running behind. I needed to go, but how could I just run out on my dying grandmother? In overextending myself, I had not considered the need for an abrupt exit. I couldn't do anything right.

The distant clouds were building—a bubbling, brewing mass. Tendrils of judgment reached out from within, seizing me, filling me with noxious, corrosive guilt. After kissing my grandmother good-bye, I slowly backed out the door. Once in the hall, I rushed for the exit; a courtesy phone hanging on the wall caught my eye. I stopped to make a quick call.

"Hi there," I managed through the lump of tears I swallowed. "Yes, I'm coming. I know I'm late. I'm sorry. I stopped by the hospital for a quick visit with Grandma." The panic in the voice on the other end of the line told me Brenda, a member of my family, was frustrated and worried everything would not get done in time. "I'm leaving the hospital right now, Brenda,"

I explained. "Don't worry; I'll be there as quickly as I can. We'll get all the work done, and your house will look beautiful; you'll see." Hanging up the phone, I lamented not spending more time with Grandma, yet I was torn because Brenda needed me as well. I seemed to live my life from this dilemma: letting down one person to please another while never even considering self-care or the fact that I had physical limitations of my own.

I nearly stumbled in my rush out the door, hurrying as though my very life depended on me being prompt, yet I was already late. I allowed Brenda's worry to compound my own anxiety as the menacing storm cast a frigid chill of self-doubt over my frantic movements.

Steadying my hand, I crammed the key into the ignition and darted out into traffic, certainly not at the safest speed. *Today is going to be a killer!* I sent up a quick, pleading prayer: "Please God, help me hold it together. People are relying on me; give me the strength to do all I need to do."

Pulling into Brenda and Tom's driveway, I was greeted by the thrashing of throw rugs. Brenda was taking out her frustration on each thoroughly beaten mat. I cringed, my stomach lurching into my throat, as I fought the devastating anxiety I experienced whenever I felt I let someone down.

Plastering on a cheerful face, I nervously jumped from the minivan, desperately trying to look happy and energetic. "So, where can I start?" I said in my perkiest voice, hoping to lighten the tension.

With Brenda's list in hand, I frantically set about my assigned tasks. Little did anyone know that my volunteering to help her was not simply a matter of my generosity. Although I did not want to admit it, even to myself, I was not as altruistic as that. Deep inside, I knew I was here to find validation, confirmation that I was okay and worthy of love. My need for approval had escalated since I had become ill. The more I found myself unable to do, the lazier and less important I felt. But today I was needed; I was given a great opportunity to feed my shriveling, anorexic self-esteem.

Unfortunately, the day was already headed south. That much-needed nourishment was being yanked farther and farther out of reach, not just by my circumstances but by the fury of the impending storm. Having arrived late, I was certain that Brenda, who was already stressed over the arrival of out-of-town family for Thanksgiving, was now equally frustrated with me. Compensating for my grave mistake in spending extra time with my dying grandmother, I determined to work extra fast and industriously. Thankfully, my energy was up. Unfortunately, that was due to adrenalin. Though it would get me through for a while, I knew my stamina would ultimately end in a disabling crash.

As I wrapped up the last bit of dusting, Tom, Brenda's husband, walked in with my sons. He had graciously offered to pick them up and even keep our youngest busy until the others got out of school, providing Brenda and me uninterrupted opportunity to prepare their home.

Double-checking my list, I inspected the house one last time for anything I might have missed. Satisfied that I was finished with a job well done, and in record time, I began to breathe a bit easier. The ominous clouds that hovered over the horizon seemed to dissipate ever so slightly, giving me a slim edge in the fight for my mental well-being. Feeling encouraged, I was ready to head out to the backyard to get some of my own work done. Hopefully, I would even be able to squeeze in a little play time with the three little guys who had stolen my heart.

Brenda and Tom were blessed with a backyard much larger than they could ever fully use, so they graciously allowed me space on the side of the house for my woodworking. My booth at the boutique where I sold various handmade country crafts that were popular at that time was low on inventory. I would have to work very hard over the next few weeks to get caught up and be prepared for the Christmas rush.

"Brenda, Tom just got here with the boys. I'm taking them out back to play while I get some patterns drawn before Scott gets here," I hollered as I corralled the rambunctious trio out the back door. Brenda thanked me for my hard work and assured me all was fine, saying she would quickly wrap up the last of the dishes before they left for the airport.

Empowered by the joy I always found in being with my boys, my heart reveled in the ray of hope now bursting through the cloudy darkness. I was delighted to capture a few moments to play with my sons. At his urging, I gave a boost to the youngest of my three cowboys as they climbed the giant grapefruit tree to defend their imaginary fort stationed within its branches. After taking a few shots from a surprisingly accurate finger gun, I feigned death, giving quite a performance, if I do say so myself. Soon my little guy grew tired of sitting in the make-believe tree fort and jumped into my arms. A game of "Tickle Monster" enthusiastically ensued. Quickly abandoning their cowboy characters for a much livelier game with "Monster Mom," his older brothers joined the chase that gleefully ended in a tangled heap of arms and legs, topped off with peals of laughter.

Glancing at my watch, that demanding sergeant on my wrist, I realized I was running behind yet again. With a sigh of regret, I tore myself away from the huddle of love. I treasured these stolen moments with our precious sons; they were growing up so quickly. I relished every opportunity to capture such tender and teachable moments.

Before rushing to my work bench, I shifted the boys' attention to their G.I. Joes hiding in the grass. At my station, I quickly cleared away the stack of wood I had left the day before. *I am so far behind I'll never catch up!* The cruel reminder resonated through my awareness like a clap of ominous thunder. Kicking it into gear, a reflex from the wearisome prompt, I determined to hurry. Scott would be here any minute. Always helpful, he often assisted me by cutting out patterns I would draw on the wood, relieving me of the work with the potentially dangerous saw and the dusty mess it produced. He had set this time aside to help me today, but I had nothing lined up for him to cut.

In a frenzy, I grabbed my pencil and tore through my patterns, rushing to trace them as quickly and accurately as humanly possible. Accusations, repeats of this morning's charge that I was not capable of managing my time, tore at my heart, a wound fashioned by the cutting edge of a polar gust. The rapidly gathering clouds began to overtake the fleeting rays of joy and hope from the momentary reprieve I'd enjoyed with my sons.

Just then Tom rounded the corner. I was so startled that I jumped, nearly dropping my pencil. I was on my last nerve. I sighed with relief when I saw that it wasn't Scott. Clearly, I was not ready for him.

"Brenda would like you to come back into the house to finish up the dishes like she asked you," Tom carefully chided me as he relayed the odd request.

"What? Brenda told me *she* was finishing them," I said rather loudly, as the stress of the day joined the raucous thunder of the encroaching mental storm, each strumming relentlessly at that last nerve.

"I'm just telling you what she said," he finished in a retreat, not wanting to be caught in the middle of two completely stressed-out women.

With that last nerve rapidly fraying, I waited until I was sure Tom was gone before I gave full rise to my frustration and threw my pencil as far as I could. In a childish fit, I stomped my way up to the house. Fueled by the fury of the gathering gale, my tirade began: *This is just great! I'm trying to make life easier for certain people, doing everything humanly possible, and what does it get me? Certainly not any appreciation! Why do I even bother? Besides, she told me she was doing the dishes!* My inner fuming continued as I gave myself over to my angry tempest.

Entering the house, I made certain to steer clear of Brenda, dodging any possible confrontation. Though I was angry, conflict was something I avoided at all costs. Instead, I did what came all too easily and at great personal expense: I swallowed my toxic rage and went to work.

It's a miracle the dishes remained in one piece as I exacted my revenge on something I knew could not return my anger. Brenda and Tom popped their heads into the kitchen to say good-bye and ask me to lock up when I left. They were headed for the airport. Then, as if things could not get any worse, Scott walked in. *Oh no, is there anything else that can go wrong today?* I cried to myself, now on the verge of tears as my anger evaporated in a haze of defeat.

"Hi, hon," my cheerful but exhausted husband greeted me. He planted a quick kiss on my cheek as he was playfully tackled by our three little guys, excited to see their daddy. Attempting to plaster on that ever-fading "everything is great" grin, I kissed him back. "Let's get out there and cut out what you've drawn. I'm tired, hungry, and in desperate need of a shower," Scott urged.

Following him out, I winced inside. I hadn't gotten much done before I was interrupted. "Where are all the pieces you drew? I only see a couple," Scott said as he carefully dug through the wood I had stacked on the work bench.

"Well, the day didn't go as I had planned ... and I only got these few done." I threw out those last few words quickly, hoping he'd somehow miss them. The disappointment on his face clearly told me he hadn't. "I'm really sorry; I can draw a few more while you cut these out," I added, desperately struggling to protect my fragile sense of worth. A disparaging fog of disappointment had suddenly rolled in, all but smothering me.

"No, let's just go home. There's not enough work here to make it worthwhile," Scott said as the boys cheered, excited to get home as well.

I was shattered. Surely Scott was now unhappy with me too. All I wanted was to bring a little pleasure and ease into the lives of others and feel good about myself in the doing, but it backfired, as it had most days. The foreboding storm, with all its dark and painful accusations, hovered ever closer as I drove the minivan home, following Scott in his faithful, paint-encrusted truck.

Scott nearly tripped over the clutter of toys and clothes that littered the floor as he walked across the threshold. "It's too bad you were helping Brenda all day when our own place looks like this," he said, completely unaware of the devastating impact his simple, truthful words carried. He was, of course, oblivious to the raging inner turmoil I was so adept at hiding. *He's right, you know; this place looks like a cyclone hit the city dump! Your house is always filthy; you are such a failure! You let your own husband and your kids down. No, not just them, you let everyone down!*

The storm made landfall.

Pummeled by its gale-force winds, my faltering sense of self was in tatters. All I had fought to believe about myself—that I was a good person; a loving mother; a devoted wife; a competent, capable woman; and most of all, that I was okay—was in shreds. I stood rejected and exposed in the acrid downpour of my own self-abasement.

Scraping up the dregs of my reserves, determination pulsed through my veins. I faced the fiery onslaught of inadequacies head-on in a last-ditch effort to confront the evil squall hell bent on my destruction. *I can clean this mess; I can make our home comfortable for Scott and the boys. I just need to get to their room and start cleaning.* Slowly, on unsteady legs, I made my way down the hall to the boys' bedroom. The determination to redeem myself drew me forward. Stepping into the room our three sons shared, my resolve faltered. The living room paled in comparison to this major disaster.

My feeble legs only carried me but a few steps before giving way, dropping me into the midst of the mayhem. I was suddenly barely aware of my surroundings. My mind was engulfed in a heavy fog of confusion, an uncertainty that rolled in on the heels of that acid rain of self-degradation. I could no longer register a complete thought. Sitting there surrounded by the fruits of my previous inactivity, I was suddenly swept up in a cyclone, not unlike Dorothy Gale of Kansas—only mine was a twister of despair. Helplessly carried away by a force much greater than I could manage, my mind screamed out as fragments of it were ripped away by the fierce, cutting winds.

In spite of my incoherence, I somehow fought on. My hands shook so badly I could barely control their movements. Trying desperately to fend off the incapacitating defeat, I set about the only task I could comprehend: making piles. Not a logical, rational, organized sorting of items—just piles. With all access cut off to the reasoning part of my brain, I had no idea what these mounds were about, only that I needed to make piles. It was as though my life depended on forming piles, even though these hapless heaps made absolutely no sense. But, in some strange, soothingly significant way, they mattered to me. From a place deep inside, a spot mysteriously protected from the storm, hope emerged: *I am accomplishing something. Maybe I am okay after all.*

In that brief moment of clarity there was a glimmer of optimism that I was possibly okay. This glimmer, however, was just as quickly extinguished as I again caught sight of that sergeant on my wrist: six o'clock. Without any real comprehension, it registered that dinner was demanded.

Obediently abandoning my beloved piles, I crawled to the wall, seeking support as I struggled to stand. Clinging to the walls, holding tightly to whatever I could grasp, I battled my way to the kitchen as though walking through a hurricane. The powerful, deadly winds ripping apart my inner world had somehow breached an unseen boundary; they were exacting their revenge outwardly as well. I was barely able to put one foot in front of the other. Somehow I eventually stumbled my way into the kitchen.

Torrential rains now accompanied the lethal wind; the landscape of the kitchen was no longer recognizable through my disoriented sight. Standing there, unsure of where I was, I had no clue as to what to do. A spark of comprehension hit when my eyes rested upon a sack of potatoes sitting on the counter. I dove for those potatoes, embracing them tightly as though they were a lifeline, an anchor in this raging storm. Relief began to wash over me. Another flicker of hope peeked through the angry clouds. I was going to make it! *I know potatoes. I can make dinner. Everything will be okay.*

Led by a glimmer of tenuous hope, I opened the utensil drawer in search of the peeler. Fear and confusion slammed against me with tsunami-like force as I stared unblinkingly into the suddenly unfamiliar jumble of gadgets. My tentative foothold and flimsy hope of survival dissolved in the wake of the mighty wave. Desperate to survive, the last vestiges of determination slowly trickled their way to my brain. A tiny spark lit my frontal lobe as one final remnant of thought flickered: *find ... potato ... peel ...*

With that concluding cognizance, I succumbed to the last of the deadly waves. Sweeping all awareness and discernable thought into its murderous undertow, it dragged me into its cold sea of emptiness. Completely spent, I collapsed. Sinking to the floor, I surrendered myself to the suffocating depths of nothingness. The perfect storm that had ominously loomed, creeping ever closer moment by moment, had ultimately claimed its victory.

# *Surrender*

SCOTT

Dr. Morrison's words filled me with dread. As I pulled out of the hospital parking lot, his disturbing and uncertain prognosis replayed itself like a broken record in my mind: *"Sandy has had a severe mental and emotional break ... I can't make any guarantees at this point; it's too early to tell ... You need to prepare yourself because Sandy might never be the same again."*

"Oh, God!" I cried out. "I honestly don't know if I can cope with this. Everything is so uncertain and chaotic. Lord, please heal Sandy; give the staff the wisdom to know how to help her. And help me. I need your strength, God; please encourage me and give me hope."

The hope and encouragement I longed for did not come. As I drove, I revisited my conversation with Dr. Morrison, desperate to find some shred of hope in what he said. He had not ruled out a full recovery, but he did not sound very optimistic, either. I know he did not want to offer me false hope, but I desperately needed to hear that Sandy would be okay. Deep inside, I knew the reason he didn't: because she might not be. Realizing this, my sense of dread only intensified. My attempts to encourage myself were met with greater discouragement. I couldn't find anything hopeful about our situation.

In my spirit I knew that God was in control and I believed that everything would work out, but in my heart I feared the worst. A battle between my thoughts and feelings quickly ensued, leaving me deeply conflicted.

The remainder of my commute was cloaked in an ominous fog of despair. I do not clearly remember arriving at my destination, but somehow I made it. Exhaustion overwhelmed me as I pulled into Tom and Brenda's driveway. I quickly filled them in on Sandy's condition and thanked them for their prayers as I loaded the boys into the car. The void created by the empty seat beside me filled the car with a foreboding loneliness as my sons rode home without their mother and I without my wife.

Putting the last of the dinner dishes in the dishwasher, I dried my hands and walked into the family room to spend some time with our sons. Although I was present physically, my mind was miles away with Sandy at the hospital. With their LEGOS to occupy them, I was thankful the boys did not notice my distraction or worry.

Although I have always appreciated the warmth and love Sandy brought to our family, the truth of greeting card notions about mothers being the heart of the home suddenly struck me. Our family was not the same in her absence.

The lonely evening dragged on. Even the encouragement I received while updating family and friends did nothing to ease my melancholy. Settling the boys into the beds of their shared room had been no easy task. I knew they missed their mother and worried about her; this fact was beginning to show in their fighting and acting out. After an hour of breaking up fights and eliminating a myriad of excuses not to sleep, I was relieved as quiet finally settled over our home, replacing the chaos. As I headed off to my own lonely bed, I braced myself for yet another restless night and the battle with my thoughts that was certain to ensue.

Sure enough, as soon as my head hit the pillow, panic and desperation overtook me; emotions I tenaciously avoided during the day, like a relentless boxer, freely pummeled me at night. Adrenalin surged through my veins, overloading my nervous system, making it impossible to lie still. I wanted to literally get up and run. I felt driven to do something, anything, to fix our problems. The trouble was, there was nothing I could do. I was completely powerless to fix Sandy. I had no control. I wasn't used to feeling this degree of helplessness. This crisis was much bigger than I could handle, and it felt as though it was too big for the doctor and hospital staff as well. I knew, however, that it wasn't too big for God. So again, I went to him for help.

*Lord, I'm scared. I'm not sure Sandy will recover, and that terrifies me. What if she doesn't? What about the kids? What about me? What am I going to do? I want to help her, but there's really nothing I can do. I don't have a lot of faith in the hospital staff right now, even though I know they are one of the best; but I have faith in you, God. I believe that you are going heal her. You have to! I just can't believe that you brought us this far just to let all our plans and dreams slip away. God, help Sandy. Restore her to the woman she was before her breakdown. Lord, just please fix the woman I love.*

Finding some level of comfort from my prayer, my nerves settled just enough to allow me to drift off to sleep. Throughout the night, however, my exhausted mind continued to plead its case to God. Then, sometime in the early morning hours, I was abruptly awakened. I sat up, attempting to clear the sleepy fog from my head. That was when I heard it. It was as clear as if God were sitting in the bed next to me. Although his voice was not audible, I heard him nonetheless.

"No, Scott. I'm going to fix *you.*"

*What? God, is that you? Wait a minute, did I hear you right? Fix me? Have you even been listening to my prayers? In case you haven't noticed, I'm not the one in the hospital. "No. I'm going to fix you." What's up with that? What about Sandy? Surely you are going to help her.*

I was more than a little irritated. Naturally, if I were actually to hear something from God, I would prefer it to be a little more encouraging and hope filled. Perhaps something like: "Scott, I have heard your prayers. Don't worry; I've got it covered. I feel your pain. Your efforts have not gone unnoticed. And because of your faith and my love for you and Sandy, I will answer your prayers and make her as good as new. Just hang tight. Help is on the way."

Too frustrated with God's response to go back to sleep, I decided to get up and prepare for another double-duty day as Mr. Mom. As I dressed, I struggled with what I'd heard… or what I thought I heard. *Was it just a nightmare? How do I know that was really God's voice? Maybe it was just my fears speaking. Yes, that's it, the voice of my fear.* Doubting my early morning encounter with God, I decided to repeat my plea. This time I verbalized it, hoping the addition of my voice would carry more weight.

"Lord, thank you that you are all powerful and almighty. Nothing is too big for you. I know you can heal Sandy. Thank you for your love for us and the fact that you want what is best for our family. I know that you also want what is best for Sandy, so please heal her and bring my wife back to me."

I was impressed with my prayer and my diplomatic approach. It seemed like a can't-lose tactic. How could God argue with that? I anxiously awaited his response as I tied my shoes. Hearing nothing more, I decided to make a pot of coffee, hoping the rich aroma would soothe my frustrations and rouse my groggy senses.

Suddenly, out of nowhere, I heard it again. "No, Scott. I'm going to fix *you.*"

Now fully awake, I was certain I had heard the Lord right the first time. However, I was not so certain he understood my prayer, so I further argued my case. "God, right now I'm not the one who needs fixing, Sandy does! So thanks for the thought, but just take care of her and I'll be fine. How about we get back to me later?"

No sooner were the words out of my mouth than again I heard: "No, Scott. I'm going to fix *you.*"

No matter how many times I rephrased my request or how many different ways I presented it, God's response remained the same. My battle with him continued for what felt like weeks but in reality was only days. Eventually, with a sincere resolution, I surrendered to God's declaration and let go of my own agenda. "Okay, God," I finally surrendered, "I'll do it your way. I don't know what it is that you intend to change in me, but I trust you to do what you know is best."

The instant I yielded to God, giving him full reign to work in my life without any resistance or interference on my part, I felt a huge burden lift.

# SURVIVAL SKILL FUNDAMENTAL

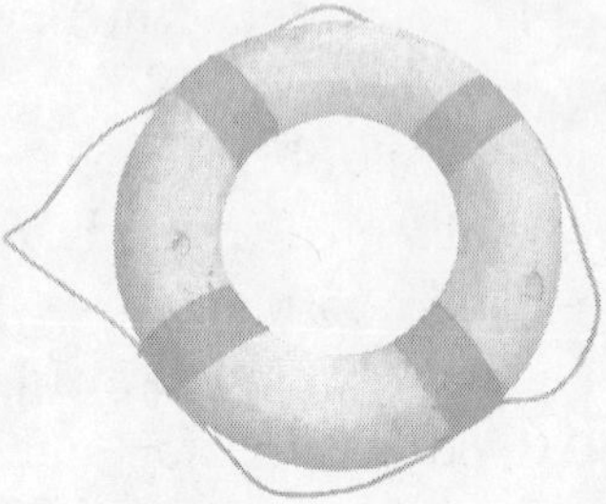

## *Leverage Your Catalyst*

SCOTT AND SANDY

Hardships and suffering are typically initiated by a catalyst, an event or individual whose disruptive presence invades and upends our lives. Sandy's breakdown was a major catalyst for our family that brought about many personal modifications and redirections. While God obviously used this catalyst to initiate positive changes in her, God also used Sandy's brokenness to change me in ways I would never before have realized. We can honestly say that the people we are today are the much-improved versions of the people we used to be. Though we would never want to relive that experience, we would not trade it, either.

God commonly uses a catalyst as an initiator, or at times what feels more like an igniter of change, rocketing us in a different direction. In James 1:2–4 we are told that God uses our challenges as catalysts to cause us to "become mature and well-developed, not deficient in any way" (MSG).

A catalyst can present itself in the form of a person or circumstance, but regardless of how it manifests, when that catalyst enters our lives it is often quite disruptive. When this harbinger of change first appears, it usually catches us off guard and can be quite upsetting. When we don't understand the true purpose of our catalyst, we react against it as if it were an enemy to be fought.

God's goal is to use our catalyst to generate positive outcomes in our life. Therefore, it is an opportunity he wants us to leverage, or work to our advantage, rather than an adversary to be avoided or eradicated. How each of us responds to our catalyst determines what the actual outcome will be. If we resist it and choose to be rigid and unyielding, a catalyst can bring about bitterness, resentment, and distrust in God. Reacting this way will keep us stuck in an often miserable existence. If, on the other hand, we realize its purpose and are flexible and teachable, we can more easily cooperate with what God is doing through our catalyst, thus activating its life-changing potential.

When we recognized our problems and struggles as catalysts for positive change, it was easier to make the choice to yield to God's work in our lives and let go of the urge to fight. Making this shift to cooperate with God's plan was crucial. It was a major turning point for us. We began to move out of the initial victimized phase in which we were stuck and into freedom, growth, understanding, and healing.

Although our new insights enabled us to view our situation differently, change and growth were still a painful process. As in childbirth, new life is brought forth from the pain we bear, making it worth the sacrifice.

As we previously stated, our initial catalyst was Sandy's breakdown, but as time went on, we discovered that behind this initiator of change there was yet another catalyst: the abuse and betrayal by a trusted family member. God used the crucial role that person played in our lives as a means to work extraordinary changes. We have chosen, for obvious reasons, not to identify this individual. Therefore, as our story continues you will find this person referred to as "Cat," an abbreviated version of "catalyst."

We would like to offer you a personal challenge. Take a moment and see if you can identify any catalyst in your life. It may be another person's actions or a difficult circumstance you are facing. Then ask yourself how God might be using this person or situation to bring about positive change in you. If you have been fighting against your catalyst, we invite you to accept it and allow it to do God's intended work.

Caution: We are not referring here to any dangerous situation. If you find yourself in an abusive or otherwise harmful or unsafe position, use wisdom and protect yourself. It may be necessary for you to remove yourself from that environment.

Listen to the advice James gives in James 1:4: "So don't try to get out of anything prematurely. Let it (*your catalyst*) do its work so you become mature and well-developed, not deficient in any way" (MSG, emphasis ours). There are no shortcuts to lasting change.

We invite you to view your perceived obstacle as an opportunity for change. This choice will create less resistance on your part and allow God the freedom to bring about the positive changes that will move you beyond your struggles.

# *Trapped*

SCOTT

"Hello," I answered breathlessly, having sprinted to the phone from the boys' room, where I was helping them clean.

"Hello, Mr. Tremp, this is Rita from the hospital. Dr. Morrison would like to meet with you tomorrow at noon to discuss a concern regarding Sandy."

"A concern? Did he say what's wrong?"

"No. He didn't say, but I'm sure he will share that with you tomorrow."

"Is Sandy okay?" I asked as my worry mounted.

"Yes, she's fine."

"Is there any way I could discuss this with him over the phone right now?" I pushed, trying desperately to get an answer now; I didn't know if I could wait another day.

"No, he specifically stated that he wanted to talk with you in person tomorrow."

Reluctantly, I replied, "Okay, tell him I will be there tomorrow."

My heart sank as I slid the phone into its cradle. What could have happened that I couldn't be told over the phone? Sandy had only been hospitalized for a few days now. What could have gone wrong? My mind automatically considered the worst. Horrific images of Sandy suffering flashed through my mind. Scolding myself for letting my mind run wild, I attempted to rein in my thoughts. I headed back to the boys' bedroom, hoping that helping them pick up their messes would distract me from my frightening speculations. However, I couldn't ignore that nagging fear that something was gravely wrong. It was all I could do to hold myself back and not rush off to the hospital.

The following day I arrived at the hospital early; the anticipation about Dr. Morrison's concern was unnerving. It took every ounce of energy I could muster to keep my mind from conjuring up worst-case scenarios. The time dragged by at an agonizing pace. As the hands of the visitor-area clock leisurely inched their way toward noon, I could no longer restrain myself. I took off down the long hall toward Sandy's room. Walking through the last door on the right, I noticed Sandy and the doctor sitting at the small table, wrapping up their therapy session while she absently picked at her lunch.

"Hi, sweetheart. How are you feeling today?" I asked, trying to hide my concern and sound as cheerful as I could. I leaned over and kissed Sandy's forehead. Though I hoped for a response, I had a feeling I would not get one. She had that glazed look in her eyes again, the look I now understood to mean that she had checked out for a while. Each time I saw her this way, the doctor's dreadful words "she may never be the same again" would gnaw away at my fraying hope.

"Hello, Scott, have a seat," Dr. Morrison invited. I pulled the extra chair over to the table and joined them. He briefly shared with me how their therapy session had gone and then got right to the point. "I've had an opportunity to speak with Sandy a couple of times now, and there is one concern in particular I would like to share with you." In a hushed tone, turning toward me as if to shield our conversation from my wife, he continued. "Sandy has what I would term a 'volcano of anger' toward Cat." Pausing to let this comment sink in, he then continued. "Are you aware of any possible reasons for her to have this degree of anger in regards to Cat?"

His question caught me off guard; I needed a moment to consider it. As I pondered the past, several run-ins we'd had with this trusted family member came to mind. They were none too pleasant, to say the least. Yet I could also remember good times we'd enjoyed as well. Had those rough moments been bad enough to cause anger of that magnitude? It then hit me that this sort of anger would most likely have built over time. With that in mind, I stretched my mind farther back, searching for anything Sandy might have shared about her childhood. My mind promptly landed upon something her previous counselors had said.

As I began to voice my response, I was cut off by an unexpected and rather detached whisper from Sandy. "I'm not mad at Cat." Her comment surprised us both, as we hadn't realized that she was coherent enough to comprehend our conversation. We turned to see her staring into her lunch tray. Pausing for a moment, we waited to see if she had any more to say.

Dr. Morrison broke the silence. "Sandy is there anything more that you want to say about Cat?"

With no answer, it appeared she was finished. Doctor Morrison motioned for me to continue. "I can identify a few extreme instances that I've observed and a few more Sandy mentioned about her childhood, but I wouldn't have thought they could result in anger of this proportion. I think you're on the right path, though, because that's surprisingly similar to what her previous counselors had said."

"Well, that confirms my own conclusions," he went on. "I think it would be best that Cat not visit Sandy for a while. I'm concerned about how she might react if she were to see Cat at this time. I've already informed the nurses at the front desk that you are to be the only visitor she is to have until further notice."

I assured him I would take care of contacting Cat. With that immediate problem out of the way, he went on to explain the process of treatment he and the staff would be following in Sandy's recovery.

Feeling very protective of Sandy, I decided to stop by the nurses' station on my way out. I wanted to double-check that they had indeed been alerted that Cat was not allowed to enter this wing of the hospital. Nancy, the head nurse, assured me that Dr. Morrison had already informed them and that arrangements had been made. Comforted in knowing that Sandy was safe, I headed for the doors, praising God for his protection and for giving us a heads-up to avert a possible setback.

As I exited the hospital, the reality that this would be Sandy's new home began to sink in. This upsetting thought rekindled the dread and concern I had for my family's future. These unwelcome feelings gripped my heart the day of her breakdown and, like a merciless noose, were daily tightening their stranglehold.

Driving home, I realized that I was also apprehensive about the impending phone call to Cat. I was pretty certain this call would open a can of worms I did not want to deal with at this point.

"God, thank you that you are in control; please help me with this dreaded call I need to make."

• • •

"Daddy, how is Mommy?" "When is she coming home?" "Where is she?" "When can we see her?" The boys rattled off a rally of questions as I was getting them ready for bed that evening. The legitimacy of the questions they posed frightened me, questions that I hadn't yet allowed myself to fully acknowledge. *Wow, it's not even been three full days and they already miss their mother something awful. What will happen to them if she is never able to return?* Up until now, I had managed to distance myself from such thoughts in order to keep going and be strong for my sons. I guess deep inside I avoided these fears, concerned that they might overtake and disable me. My feelings would have to wait. The boys needed me. Sandy needed me. I had to be strong for my family. Instead, I buried my feelings and my needs under the many layers of responsibility and dedication to my family.

Suddenly gang piled by three surprisingly strong young boys, I was quickly returned to the present. A wrestling match ensued, quickly turning into our version of the "Tickle Me" game. All thoughts of sleep flew out the window, taking with them our previous concerns. Choruses of "Tickle me more, Daddy, tickle me more" rang out, as none of us wanted this favorite pastime to end. Feeling grateful for the diversion and the closeness with my sons, I romped with them until I was simply too tired to move.

As I helped them finish getting ready for bed, I was carried back to the day Sandy discovered my secret for getting the boys ready for church on Sunday mornings when she was away. Her incredulous laughter still rang in my ears. To this day, I don't know how she discovered my secret; my sons must have ratted me out.

It all began when our youngest was a toddler; our oldest would have been four. Sandy was away at a women's retreat and the difficult task of getting the three little guys fed and ready for church on time fell squarely on my shoulders. Being a typical guy, I searched for the most efficient way to accomplish this challenging task. I realized I could shave off valuable time by bathing and dressing them in their Sunday best, rather than their pajamas, the night before. Then all I had to do in the morning was get them up, feed them, comb their hair, and brush their teeth. My biggest dilemma, however, was whether or not to put their shoes on at bedtime or wait until the morning. Practicality won out. I made the decision to put their shoes on before bed. (Sandy nearly hit me when she discovered that part.)

With the exception of a few wrinkles on their matching clothes (I knew that Sandy would never have approved) and the boys each voicing their disapproval—"This isn't how mommy does it"—my plan worked like a charm! We arrived at church with plenty of time to spare. And, I must say, I felt pretty proud of myself.

Smiling as I reminisced, tears threatened to fill my eyes at the realization that Sandy wasn't here to share in this memory, which always received a shake of her head and a smile on her lovely face. I couldn't help but wonder again if our life would ever be the same.

Quickly choking back the sadness, I finished getting the boys settled into their beds and explained that Mommy would be going away for a while but that they would be able to visit her soon. Doing my best to stick closely to their normal routine, I told them one of their favorite Mr. Mole stories, a series of tales I made up that included characters comically mirroring our own family. After uproarious giggles about Baby Mole and his smelly diaper, I calmed them down and prayed with them. Kissing each one good night, I tucked the covers securely around them, cocooning them in the protection I wished I could provide for their wounded little hearts.

"Good night, boys. I love you. Mommy loves you too," I said as I walked out their door.

"Night night, Daddy," they all called out. "Night night, Mommy," three sad little voices whispered in the darkness as I continued, brokenhearted, down the hall.

With the boys safely tucked into bed, I pulled myself together and headed for the phone. It was time to fill everyone in on Sandy's progress and to face the dreaded call to Cat. As much as I was not looking forward to this call, I knew that if it would keep Sandy safe and on her way to recovery I would willingly call the devil himself. Still, I saved that conversation for last.

"Hi, Cat. I'm calling to give you an update on Sandy. She seems to be adjusting well to the hospital environment, but her doctor requested that she not have any visitors for a while," I explained, as I had with everyone else I'd called. Rather than risk hurting Cat's feelings, I extended the doctor's orders to everyone so this individual would not feel singled out.

Cat asked the question I knew would come but hoped wouldn't: "Why can't she have visitors?"

"Well"—I hesitated, feeling put on the spot—"the doctor just feels that right now it would be best for her to have no visitors other than me. I will let you know as soon as he gives the okay for visitation."

"Well, that doesn't make sense to me," Cat persisted, not used to being told what to do.

"I understand, but for Sandy's sake, let's just try to respect the doctor's judgment," I countered, rushing to end the conversation before more questions could be asked. I thanked Cat for cooperating and concluded the call with an assurance to keep Cat updated.

Glad to have that uncomfortable task crossed off my list, I checked in on our sleeping boys one last time. Retiring to my own empty bedroom, I lay down, utterly exhausted. Praying once more for strength, protection, and healing for my wounded family, I finally drifted off into another fitful night's sleep.

The following evening I received a disturbing call from Cat. Assuming Cat was calling to check on Sandy's well-being, I was taken aback when the first thing out of Cat's mouth was, "What is Sandy remembering?" What made this request so odd was that nothing had been mentioned about Sandy remembering anything. All Cat knew was what I had told everyone: that Sandy had a breakdown, was in the hospital, and was not allowed to have visitors.

Quickly regrouping my thoughts, I responded, "Nothing that I know of. Why do you ask?"

"Oh, I was just curious, that's all," Cat sheepishly replied.

After an awkward ending to an equally awkward beginning, I hung up feeling unsettled by the peculiarity of the call.

• • •

Work had been spotty lately, which was both good and bad. I really needed some downtime with all of my added responsibilities, but we also desperately needed the money. Having no work lined up, I was home the next day when the phone rang.

"Mr. Tremp, this is Nancy from the hospital. I am calling to inform you that there's been an incident."

"What do you mean an incident? What happened? Is Sandy okay?" I asked, the alarm in my voice escalating with each word.

"Yes, she is resting now."

"Well, what happened?" I insisted, frustrated that this nurse was taking forever to give me a straight answer.

"Well, um … " She hesitated, noticeably uncomfortable with what was to come. "Cat came by to see Sandy this afternoon, and Sandy had an unfavorable reaction."

"Unfavorable, what do you mean by unfavorable?"

"She ultimately had to be restrained and sedated, but she is—"

Cutting her off midsentence, my shock was quickly replaced by anger. "Restrained? Sedated! What did Cat do? How on earth did this happen?" I demanded. "I even talked with you personally about this, and you assured me that Cat wouldn't be allowed in. Dr. Morrison specifically stated the potential danger a visit from Cat could pose to Sandy's recovery. What the h*** are you guys doing down there?"

"I know, and I'm very sorry. It was a mistake," she offered, apologetically.

"I'll be right there," I said.

The receiver was already on its way to the cradle when Nancy hurriedly shouted, "Wait, Mr. Tremp?"

"I'm still here."

"You can come to the hospital, but you won't be able to see Sandy. Due to the severity of the incident we have her on twenty-four-hour lockdown for her own protection. You are welcome to visit tomorrow, but I assure you she is okay now and in good hands."

Worried about my wife and feeling utterly helpless, I negotiated, "Can I at least talk with her?"

"I'm afraid not, she is heavily sedated. I'm sure that she will be much better tomorrow. Don't worry; we are taking good care of her," the nurse offered in a feeble attempt to encourage me.

Stunned and angry, I slammed the phone down and paced the floor as I vented my frustration to a vacant room. "She's in good hands my a**! How did this happen? The hospital assured me of Sandy's safety and now this! Am I surrounded by idiots? And what the h*** was Cat thinking? I called and nicely, but clearly, asked Cat not to visit Sandy; I did all I could to prevent Cat from feeling singled out, and for what? What good did it do? It happened anyway! And, God, I thought you had this under control? How could you have allowed this to happen?"

Placing my hands on my knees, I bent over and took several deep breaths, slowly calming myself down. It took every shred of restraint within me to resist both rushing to the hospital and calling and chewing Cat out. I knew that screaming at Cat wouldn't do any good anyway. I should have known this would happen, but I thought, for Sandy's sake, Cat would respect the doctor's wishes, like everyone else had. The more I thought about what just happened, the more my anger became matched by an intense curiosity. *Why would Sandy react so? It's not like she's never seen Cat before. What's different now? What on earth could Cat have done to her? Is this that volcano of anger Dr. Morrison was talking about? It sounded more like terror than rage, from what the nurse told me.* "Lord, what's going on here?" I prayed. "Help the doctors get to the bottom of this. Be with Sandy. Enable her to feel your love and protection as she goes through this. And please keep Cat away from her."

Having calmed somewhat, I called and demanded to talk with Dr. Morrison. I made my feelings known to the good doctor, insisting that the staff do whatever it took to never allow Cat to visit again or I would be pulling Sandy out immediately. He apologized profusely and assured me extra measures would be taken to prevent this from ever happening again.

*Lord, this is becoming so bizarre,* I thought as I slumped into my chair, feeling as though I had just stepped into the *Twilight Zone.*

• • •

SANDY

*Help me! Cat's coming! Help me! Cat's coming!* The alarm sounded deep within the recesses of the mind, its siren reverberating louder and louder until the urgent cry escaped through trembling lips.

I could hear the terrified pleas for help. The voice was familiar, but it sounded so … childlike. Was it really mine? Things inside my head were so mixed up, so confused; I couldn't think. Words were coming out of my mouth, words I couldn't control, yet it all felt so distortedly normal that I didn't question it. I could see Dr. Morrison. I was looking right at him, but it was as though I was Alice peering out from inside the looking glass.

"No, Sandy, Cat is not coming. You are safe here, and everything is okay." I could hear Dr. Morrison's voice and his attempts to reassure me. I felt his hands on my shoulders, endeavoring to give comfort, but I could not fully connect with these beacons of reality. Instead, the alarm continued crying out, not stopping until it had fully exhausted its efforts.

The sound of Dr. Morrison's voice escorted me back to the present, up and out of the rabbit hole I had unknowingly slipped into. Even so, I remained in Wonderland, a place of confused and disjointed reality, where I was carried a few days earlier by the tsunami of the perfect storm.

My session was soon over. The terror that had just moments before consumed me vanished completely and was temporarily wiped from my memory. I continued through my day as though it had never happened.

A few hours later, Nancy, my therapist, came to get me for our session. We left my room and walked the long hallway, finally passing the nurses' station that sat as the watchman over the door to this wing of the hospital. Taking a left at the bench provided for visitors, we pushed through the glass doors that separated the visitors' area from a short hall that led to several small therapy rooms. Nancy chose the first door to her left; I followed her in, and we each took a seat in the two chairs provided. We were not long into our session before the strange, ominous scene repeated itself.

"Cat is coming! Help me! Cat is coming!" Once again the persistent, terrified warnings rang out. I was back in the rabbit hole. Nancy worked to convince me that I was safe within the confines of the hospital, yet nothing would quiet the disturbing cries. As before, they persisted until the fear was spent. With all emotion depleted, a surreal tranquility settled over the room as my mind deleted the episode, shielding me from the disconcerting experience.

When our session was completed, Nancy guided me out of the small room. As I turned to walk toward the glass doors, those temporarily abated fears were suddenly fully realized. This time I was not in the rabbit hole. This was reality… and Cat was here! My mind reeled in distress as alarms and sirens screamed *danger* when my eyes locked onto Cat's. The object of my fear sat calmly on the bench as though having every right to be there. A cacophony of terror shrieked the alert: *Run! Run! Run!* I turned to run, but there was nowhere to go. I was trapped in a suffocatingly small dead-end hallway. Quickly, my terror-stricken mind registered the three therapy room doors, doors that stood as sentinels, welcoming my escape. Like a caged and frightened animal, I grabbed at the handle of the nearest sentry, twisted, and pushed, but it wouldn't budge. *Run! Run! Go anywhere; just run!* In a blind panic I raced for the next door, but it was just as unyielding as the first. At the third and final door, the last promise of escape, I was met again with an unsympathetic lock. *No, let me in! Please let me in!* My growing desperation frenzied. Demanding a rescue, I kicked and beat at my unwilling champion. I couldn't accept its refusal to protect me. I had no other hope. With each pounding of my fist, I fought the defeat that threatened not only my resolve but my very life itself. I had to escape this glass-walled prison. I was too afraid to turn and look; I felt certain that Cat, my fear personified, sat silently evaluating my every move.

As the realization set in that I had no hope of physical escape, I slid down the wall into the nearby corner and hugged my knees to my chest. Closing my eyes to the all-consuming fear, I allowed my mind to lead me off to a safer place.

This momentary calm provided Nancy the opportunity she needed to gain control of the situation… or so she thought. Dropping down to my level, she reached out her hands to calm and rein in her previously hysterical patient. But at her touch I was jolted back to reality and my frantic fear shifted to an intensely distressed rage. I was suddenly aware of Nancy's presence and her now empty promise of protection. Out of my mind in agony, I screamed, "You lied! You didn't protect me! You lied!" With all rationality long gone, I mindlessly beat my head against the wall. Primal sounds of anguish and misery filled the hall as I sobbed tormented tears. "You lied! No one can protect me! I'm not safe anywhere!"

Time stood torturously still while around me the hospital was abuzz. Alerted by my screams, the nurses raced to ascertain the situation and called for the backup of additional male staff members. Once assembled, the four men stepped in. Each taking a flailing limb, they carried me unceremoniously through the visitors' area and into the nurses' station. Blind with agony, I did not see that Cat was gone. I'm not certain if there was an escort or if Cat slipped out during all the confusion, but the object of my fear had departed.

In spite of my thrashing about, I found myself hastily strapped to an unfamiliar bed in the lockdown room. Soon I could feel the eerie warmth of the sedative as the aggressive invader coursed through my veins.

Something from my past clicked. My mind quickly awakened to the familiarity of this drugged sensation. Crazed with terror, I mistakenly related the attempts to calm me with past threats to my life. *No! Don't sleep! Stay awake!* I struggled to defend myself from the encroaching drug. My already mixed-up reality was eclipsed by flashes of a frighteningly familiar past. Though the setting was different, the sensations were the same. I writhed in terror, afraid that if I succumbed to the drug's overwhelming power I would no longer be able to protect myself. It soon no longer mattered as this powerful intruder assaulted my brain cells and nerve endings, deadening them until I had nothing left to fuel my fight. The medication I perceived as life threatening quieted me into unconsciousness. The internal storm was quelled temporarily, but its devastation was far from over.

# *Homecoming*

SCOTT

"But I don't have six thousand dollars! Our insurance isn't covering any of this; it's all coming out of my own pocket. Listen, I am self-employed and work is slow right now. Can't you work with me? Isn't there any way I can make payments?"

In a very detached manner, the hospital's finance manager replied, "I'm sorry, Mr. Tremp, but unless you can pay for next week's stay by this Friday, you will need to come in and pick up your wife on the front doorstep."

"But you don't understand. Sandy is in a very fragile state. Her doctor warned that it would be damaging to remove her from the hospital at this time. Certainly you wouldn't just throw her out?"

"I'm sorry, Mr. Tremp, but there is nothing more I can do." With that, she disconnected the line.

"You've got to be kidding me!" I yelled incredulously into dead air.

Slamming the phone onto my desk, I jumped up from my office chair. *The nerve of this heartless woman! I can't believe she actually said that! A hospital is supposed to be there to help people, not throw them to the curb.*

In a more rational moment, I could have understood the hospital's position. They needed to make money, and I was the one who chose one of the most expensive places to facilitate Sandy's recovery. But right now I was not in a rational place, and that woman's insensitive comment felt completely inappropriate.

My frustration smoldered. The anger that consumed me was suddenly overshadowed by fear as my mind conjured up unsettling images of my frightened and bewildered wife sitting on the hospital's doorstep, clinging tightly to her pillow and her Bible. Shaking these disturbing yet realistic images from my mind, I offered up another of many pleas to God for help.

Fueled by desperation, I sat back down at my desk to take inventory of our available funds. Digging through various invoices and bids, I added up the money I could collect before Friday. My heart sank at the inadequate total. That amount would hardly cover our household expenses, let alone the hospital bill.

I frantically began a mental scan of the house in search of anything more I could sell. I had already sold furniture and anything else of value. The financial pressure mounted the previous week to the point that I broke down and parted with our family minivan. This was a monumental decision for me. Not only did it perfectly fit our needs, but it was the only newer vehicle we had ever paid off. This minivan represented the first milestone in our overall plan to become debt free and financially stable, a plan that was being ripped from my grasp finger by fighting finger. Because I had to sell it on such short notice, I was not even able to get the full value of our coveted automobile. To add insult to injury, the car that I bought to replace it was an old clunker that looked terrible and ran even worse. It was all I could afford. I tried to be thankful, yet all I could focus on was my own sense of failure as the provider.

I began pacing the room, my mind anxiously seeking an answer to my dilemma, but it seemed there were no real solutions. From my previous dealings with this billing manager, I had no doubt that she would make good on her threat if I didn't come up with the money by Friday. It was already Wednesday. I had no idea how I was going to produce that much cash in such a short time.

Finishing my mental inventory, it became all too clear that there was nothing of value left, other than the house itself, and there was a very real threat of losing that as well. My thoughts went to the churches, our family, and our friends who had already graciously helped. I couldn't think of anyone else to ask. I still felt the sting from the utter humiliation of having to beg others for money, some of whom where complete strangers. My back was to the wall; the proverbial well had run completely dry. Despair enveloped me with a suffocating and immobilizing intensity that threatened to shut me down. Attempting to escape this stifling sensation, I stepped out of my home office and began walking a worry path in the living room carpet. Fortunately, the kids were in school, which afforded me the opportunity to thoroughly vent my feelings as I paced.

"How am I going to come up with six thousand dollars in two days?" I bellowed in frustration, throwing my arms up to God. "Where are you when I need you most? If Sandy is supposed to be in the hospital, why must I fight so hard every single week to keep her there? Why does life have to be this difficult? I don't understand you; you always wait until everything comes right down to the wire before you finally decide to show up! The time is *now,* God. We are down to the wire, and I've got nothing. This whole situation just sucks!"

I continued, my tirade having reached a crescendo. "I know that I gave you full reign to 'fix' me, but come on, God, this is ridiculous! How much more do I have to take?"

Continuing my frantic, agitated march, I deliberated with such intensity I thought myself into a corner. I was completely out of ideas and entirely out of resources. I combed my fingers through my hair, hoping to somehow disentangle my tormenting thoughts.

Out of the blue I was struck with an idea: *If I can't raise the money to keep Sandy in the hospital, perhaps this is God's way of saying that it is time to bring her home.*

I hadn't even considered that possibility. I was so wrapped up in keeping Sandy hospitalized that the thought of bringing her home had not crossed my mind. Was this a viable option? My heart could only hope. I longed to have my wife back home and the stress of the financial pressure eased.

As I considered this prospect, a sense of excitement penetrated my cloud of desperation. I decided that first thing in the morning I would discuss my idea with Dr. Morrison. Feeling more hopeful than I had in weeks, I relaxed and tried to catch a quick nap on the couch before the boys arrived home from school. As I dozed off, I thanked God for what I hoped was his direction.

• • •

"Hello, Dr. Morrison," I began, "I was wondering if you could give me any indication as to when Sandy might be able to come home. To be honest with you, we are completely out of money and our credit cards are maxed to the limit. We are in debt as far as we can go and on the brink of financial disaster. We may even lose our house." The deafening silence on the other end of the phone lingered for what seemed an eternity as Dr. Morrison sought to find the right words.

"Scott, I need to be up front with you. Sandy is still in a very fragile state, as you well know. As I previously shared with you, in a case this severe the hospital stay is a minimum of six months. It has only been one month, so you are still looking at, at least, another five. In my professional opinion, she's not ready to come home. I'm concerned that releasing her prematurely might compromise her recovery."

I reached for the chair as I felt my knees begin to buckle. *Five more months! How in the world am I going to come up with...* My mind couldn't even begin to grasp the math on that amount of money. I didn't know how I was going to raise six thousand dollars, let alone money to cover the next five months. Torn between my desire for Sandy to get the help she so desperately needed, and my lack of resources, I reiterated to Dr. Morrison the seriousness of our financial situation. I also made sure he understood that I could not muster the money for another week's stay.

"Well," Dr. Morrison responded, finally grasping my concern and dilemma, "if we have no other choice, perhaps we can devise a plan to create a therapeutic environment in your home that will feel safe and be conducive to Sandy's recovery. But I need to be honest with you; this will not be easy on you or your family." I took his warning to heart, but at the same time, I felt relieved by this creative solution. I assured him that I would do whatever it took to help facilitate her continued care.

The next day I met with the doctor and the hospital staff to formulate an in-home treatment plan for Sandy. Since the following day was the last day of her stay, the staff was in a rush, having just one day to prepare. The arrangements they made were still expensive and well beyond our means, but the health professionals we would be working with allowed us to make payments—payments we would be making years later and feeling the repercussions of to this very day.

While the hospital finished their preparations I hurriedly readied the house. I cleaned everywhere and organized our bedroom to serve as Sandy's living space for as long as necessary. I wanted to her homecoming to be as stress free as possible.

As I settled into bed that night, exhausted from a busy day of domestic duties, I began thinking about the day to come. I was conflicted about Sandy returning home. One side of me wanted her home, but another feared I would not be able to take care of her. As I lay there conflicted, my mind was assaulted by a barrage of worry-filled, disjointed thoughts. *What did I get myself into? Sandy doesn't even want to come home. How will I continue to work, manage the house, take care of the boys, and see to Sandy's needs all at the same time?... I'm not Superman! Am I really up for this? How am I going to afford all these new appointments when I can't even cover the bills we already have? How will Sandy adjust to being at home? She is still frail and frightened,* so *unlike the woman I married. How will the boys react to her? How will she respond to them? How will she respond to me? Will the real Sandy ever come back again? What if she has to go back into the hospital again?*

Unable to untie the knots in the pit of my stomach, I called out to God for relief. After wrestling with my thoughts for a couple of hours, I finally drifted off to sleep, spending what would thankfully be my last night alone in our bed.

• • •

SANDY

"No, no, no, I can't go home yet!" I cried out in fear. Dr. Morrison, Nancy, and Scott had gathered in the doctor's office for a private meeting about sending me home. I was completely surprised and totally derailed by their decree that I would be leaving the hospital the very next morning. "How could you have this meeting without me? This isn't right. I can't go home yet. It's all too scary!" I shrieked.

"Just a minute, Sandy, you haven't heard the plan yet," Dr. Morrison gently interrupted.

"The boys will need me when I'm home; how can I possibly care for them? All that pressure! Oh, God, what will I do? You can't do this to me!" I cried, tears streaming freely down my face. I was terrified. Not knowing what to do with myself, I turned and ran back down the hall toward my room. I was desperate to flee the unjust sentence I had been handed. Collapsing on my bed in search of some much-needed comfort, I hugged my stuffed bear, a gift from Scott just four short weeks prior.

"Jesus, what am I going to do? I don't want to go. Please, Lord, I can't go home. Please don't let them send me away from here when I'm finally feeling safe." My prayer was barely audible and wracked with sobs as the terror I had begun to challenge over the last few weeks pressed in on me, threatening to overtake me yet again.

This pervasive fear had attached itself the day of my breakdown. Though the terror of Cat was at its core, the fear's loathsome tendrils invaded every part of my being like a virile cancer. The malignancy was vast and all encompassing. The prescribed medications for this disease of the spirit, beyond the pharmaceuticals, were the Scripture verses Dr. Morrison encouraged me to search out and scribe onto pages we hung on my walls.

> Greater is he that is in me than he that is in the world. (1 John 4:4)
>
> God has not given me a spirit of fear but of power, love, and a sound mind. (2 Timothy 1:7)
>
> There is no fear in love because perfect love drives out all fear. (1 John 4:18)
>
> The Lord is my refuge, a stronghold in times of trouble. (Jeremiah 16:19)
>
> The Lord is my light and my salvation—why should I be afraid? (Psalm 27:1)
>
> The Lord is close to the brokenhearted and saves those who are crushed in spirit. (Psalm 34:18)

I was seeking encouragement from these truths when Scott, Dr. Morrison, and Nancy walked in. Scott sat next to me on my bed and lovingly brushed the dampened hair from my face.

The three of them gently explained our financial state, trying not to add to my stress and fears but at the same time helping me see the reality of our situation. They encouraged me by describing the care I would continue to receive at home. Scott comforted me through his promised commitment to care for the boys while protecting me from the stresses of parenting. These reassurances eventually quelled the tide of fear that had overwhelmed me at the thought of returning home too soon. Though still afraid and certainly not at all happy about the new turn of events, I was willing to give it my best.

• • •

As Scott gently guided me across the threshold of our home, I was immersed in hungry hugs and greedy kisses that quickly overwhelmed my fragile senses. Holding the mommy-starved boys back proved too difficult a task for our friend who watched them so Scott could bring me home. The boys were beside themselves with joy at having me home after what must have seemed like an eternity. I too was happy to be reunited with my family, but I was overcome by the instant chaos of high-pitched voices and the rough-and-tumble love being thrown my way. Tears of distress began to cloud my eyes as I fought to keep them from falling. Scott, recognizing my duress, asked our friend to distract the boys long enough for him to get me into bed, where the world felt safer and more manageable.

What I feared would happen was already coming to fruition. I loved my sons too much to simply brush them off. Part of me wanted to give my boys the love and attention they needed, while the other side was completely overwhelmed at the thought of such a daunting task. So I lay alone in bed with my tears, weeping over my divided heart, completely unable to rest. I wondered if this in-home treatment would work. I fought against feeling trapped. I couldn't go back to the hospital. We simply could no longer afford it, yet this new situation was already proving to be overwhelming and scary.

I soon dried my tears and summoned my strength for a short visit with the boys. I asked Scott to bring our sons into the room, as I decided that I would appease the half of me that wanted to see them, since neither part of me had any peace the way things currently stood. Sheepishly they each entered, crawling up onto the bed to be near me. Scott made his way to his side of the large mattress, joining our reunion. We were a family again.

The boys began updating me on their young lives. They each shared interesting stories from school and the time they had spent at friends' houses. Pulling up pant legs and shirt sleeves, they revealed their latest scabs and scars, badges of honor from recent falls. I was also treated to a parade of LEGOS—jets and boats they had recently created.

Sadly for them, most of what they wanted to share went unsaid as the strain of the gathering took its toll on me. So began a policy for the boys that would hold true for the next few months: brief moments with Mommy followed by an admonition to leave the room and play quietly. I am not sure which had been more difficult—for them to have me completely absent, or have me within reach but with no real access.

Much of my time was spent alone in my room with my Bible, my bear, and my journal. The emotionally fragile state I was in had me functioning at more of a childlike level than that of an adult. The isolation, though good for my overwrought nervous system, was often difficult. I felt lonely. Scott stayed with me as much as his other responsibilities would allow. Yet no matter how much time he gave me, Scott's loving presence was not enough to soothe the fear and intense inner pain. Nothing brought relief—not Scott, not the medications, not the Scriptures, not even our prayers.

I spent many hours releasing a storehouse of long-forgotten tears. The anguish was primal. The pain was intense. The fear was immobilizing. I was consumed by this emotional torrent, a downpour of pain I was not sure I could bear.

I wanted to no longer exist. I wanted to vanish, disappear, evaporate into nothingness.

I no longer felt God's presence. This was a desolate place I had entered.

Scott encouraged me to write out my thoughts and feelings. I began journaling through my distress, my words often digressing to scribbled red and black images when no words could express my pain.

I also recorded the memories that dropped in and out of my mind. Fragmented and distorted pictures, sensations, or even smells would shoot through my senses, often too quickly for me to comprehend. Nonetheless, I put pen to paper with everything I experienced, even the most insignificant detail. I drew pictures and cut out words and photos from magazines that best represented my mental confusion, creating collages of anguish. We hoped these visual aids would help us piece together this mysterious puzzle of mine and eradicate the cancerous fear that had consumed me.

Scott had taken as much time off work as our budget would allow, yet I was not well enough to be left alone. To solve this problem, Scott devised yet another clever plan. In the mornings he got the boys ready and off to school. Then he would leave for work as usual, only now with me in tow. Once at the job site, he created a safe, comfortable spot for me to sit or lie down near the area where he would be working. Fortunately, most of the homes he painted were vacant, providing me the opportunity to be with Scott while he worked without drawing undue attention to myself. Maintaining privacy was essential. We never knew when a fresh torrent of tears would consume me or when I would be hit out of nowhere with unsubstantiated fear. At those times I was lost to my pain and needed to be re-grounded in the present. Scott was my anchor who brought me back to the here and now, planting my emotional feet on more solid ground. This work arrangement was difficult for us both, but it kept me close to my lifeline while allowing him to generate an income.

It is a wonder Scott was able to get any work done with all the interruptions he faced, but his aptitude for making things happen somehow got us through. His work week was continually disrupted. There were my daily appointments with either Dr. Morrison or my new therapist to work around. Our youngest needed to be picked up from kindergarten at noon on the days when our helpful friends were not available. Between the two of us, we kept Scott very busy.

On days when our five-year-old was with us, he and I busied ourselves by creating various costumes for him out of Scott's supply of masking paper and tape. One moment he was a cowboy with chaps and a belt. An empty roll of paper, bent and secured with tape, suddenly transformed into a Colt 44. After depleting another roll, a Ninja would appear, revealing only his eyes as he wielded a sword made of the empty tubes. Even Superman with an S of tape on the front of his shirt and a cape of indestructible masking paper entered our repertoire. Scott was treated to a show of each character, often resulting in cheers of laughter at our son's creative antics. These times were actually quite therapeutic, a welcome distraction from my inner turmoil and created special memories for the three of us.

Scott maintained an exhausting pace for nearly a year, working as much as he could in spite of the added responsibilities and deleted hours from his workday. This increased load made it necessary for him to withdraw from school. He had begun his post-graduate studies in counseling the previous year and was greatly anticipating abandoning his painting, exchanging it for the rewarding opportunity to help others once again. Though this all must have taken a great toll on him, he never complained. I was able to stay out of the hospital, and he said he considered that most important of all. I am eternally grateful for all the sacrifices Scott made on my behalf during these rough times. His willingness to go to those dark places with me, his ability to persevere and keep going in spite of his own pain, was nearly a supernatural feat. He is my hero. My love, respect, and gratitude for his willingness to make such difficult sacrifices can never fully be expressed; they are too vast for words.

# *From Bad to Worse*

SANDY

My initial meeting with Julie came the week of Christmas. I found her warm and caring. Feeling comfortable with her right away, a trust soon developed between my new counselor and me. This trust, however, began to quickly dissolve when Julie announced that Cat was her client as well and had come in to the office expressing a desire to see me. I was shocked. The terror I worked so hard to diminish while in the hospital threatened to overcome me as Julie seemed to press me to reconnect with Cat. Scott, my ever-present lifeline, stepped in and helped me explain to Julie that I was terrified of Cat and was in no way ready for a face-to-face meeting.

Under the protective eye of Nancy and Dr. Morrison, I met with Cat prior to being released from the hospital. This meeting was part of their overall program to uncover the root of and help me deal with my intense fear and anger in connection to Cat. My previous reaction still did not make any sense to us. My fears were very real, but there was nothing substantial on which I could base them. We felt that if I met with Cat in a protective environment I could get to the bottom of these emotions. However, no hidden insights were uncovered in the short meeting and nothing was resolved. I was still burdened with my extreme and unmanageable fear.

Meeting with Cat in this new environment was a completely different situation altogether. Outside of the hospital walls, in spite of Scott's efforts to shield me, I was dealing with many physical, emotional, and mental pressures. Without full access to my faculties, due to my fractured mental state, I could not muster up the courage or the ability to feel safe around Cat at this point.

I left Julie's office feeling the worst I'd felt since returning home. Scott offered reassurances to my fears while we both sat in confusion over the questions this conversation elicited: How did Cat and I end up at the same counselor? Why was Cat seeing a counselor in the first place? Cat had not normally been one to seek help.

I was apprehensive about going back to Julie's, scared I might run into Cat in the office or even that I might have to continue to convince Julie that I was not ready for such a confrontation. Scott encouraged me to give it one more chance. He also reminded me that Julie had promised to schedule my appointments on a different day than Cat's. Drawing strength from Scott's conviction, I mustered the courage to walk into Julie's office.

*Oh, no! Not again!*

There in the waiting room sat Cat! In spite of my best efforts to protect myself, this person kept turning up. I felt as though I was in some torturous time warp, destined to repeat these upsetting encounters. I clung to Scott like a frightened child, using him as a shield to protect me. Walking through the waiting room, maneuvering in such a way as to stay between Cat and me, Scott made his way back into Julie's office with me glued to his side. Not stopping to knock on the slightly ajar door, he protectively ushered me inside.

"What is Cat doing here?" I squeaked, barely holding it together as I tentatively dropped my shaking body into the nearest chair.

"We talked about getting you two together to work things through," Julie explained.

"Yes, we talked about it, but I emphatically stated that I was not ready for it!" I retorted, clutching Scott's hand for much-needed support, surprising myself at the ability to stand for myself in my current state.

"I think you should see Cat for a few minutes. Then we can have the rest of the session alone," Julie encouraged.

"No! I can't do that now!" I said with surprising assertiveness, in spite of the all-consuming fear.

"Then I guess I need to let Cat know that you won't meet today," Julie said with what I perceived as a hint of annoyance in her voice.

"I'm so scared, Scott," I cried after Julie left, closing the door behind her.

"It's okay, hon; you did great. I'm proud of you for standing for yourself and saying what you need to. Don't worry; it will all work out," Scott encouraged in spite of the death grip I had on his hand.

A few moments later, Julie re-emerged, but not with intentions to begin our session, as I had hoped. Instead she came with yet another message from Cat. "Sandy, Cat took the afternoon off work, rearranging a schedule to be here, and feels you should reconsider."

"Absolutely not!" I cried through clenched teeth as I strained to hold myself together, my anger outrunning my fear. I mistakenly assumed that my initial stance would have sufficed, but it seemed I needed to gird myself for battle. "Please go out there and tell Cat I will not meet today!" I said, exasperated that my emphatic denial was not enough for either of them.

When Julie returned again she shared that Cat had left very angry and upset that I refused our meeting. Although I was frustrated with Julie for putting me in this difficult situation, my overall brokenness and confusion triumphed, and by the end of the session I decided to give Julie yet another chance.

On the way home Scott asked me if I wanted to find another counselor. Everything already felt so overwhelming that the thought of searching for someone new, filling them in on my situation, and adjusting to their style created more stress for me than staying with Julie at this point, so I chose to stay.

SCOTT

I was concerned. I questioned whether Sandy's best interests were taking priority. Based on Sandy's reactions to Cat, I didn't feel a meeting at this point was wise. The last thing I wanted was for Sandy to end up back in the hospital. Cat's uncanny ability to manipulate caused me to wonder if we should search for another counselor. I was doubly confused that Julie had come so highly recommended by the hospital staff. Since Sandy had a high degree of trust in the staff's recommendation, abandoning their suggestion would be difficult for her. I knew Sandy was still in a fragile state, and she had expressed how overwhelming finding a new therapist would be at this point. I believed that, as much as possible, the choice of Sandy's counselor had to be her own. Nevertheless, I was concerned that she was not in a place to make this decision alone. "God," I prayed, "speak to Sandy. Help her make the best decision possible. If it is to find herself a new therapist, then help her feel safe and comfortable with this change."

SANDY

As my work with Julie progressed, we were finally breaking ground on my issues—sorting through my memories, searching for an answer to my pervasive fear. After a few sessions she again pushed another meeting with Cat. I did not understand Julie's approach. It felt as though smoothing things over with Cat was more important to her than getting underneath my emotional pain, disjointed memories and images. Perhaps Julie felt the best way to overcome that fear was to face it, but I was terrified of Cat and not ready for such a direct approach. I also realized I needed to move beyond this fear if I was ever going to get better. Besides, I did not like feeling this way concerning Cat. There had to be a way to work through this. So, in spite of Scott's concerns and advice to the contrary, I soon acquiesced and we began working toward a meeting with Cat. Though hesitant, Scott supported my decision.

A few short weeks went by and the meeting was scheduled. Facing my fears was excruciating, but in this meeting I proved to myself that I could be in the same room with Cat without completely falling apart. I still felt uneasy and fearful around Cat. Something just did not seem right, even though I could not put my finger on it. At the conclusion of the session with Cat, Scott and I approached the desk to make my next appointment. Cat reached the receptionist first and, unaware of our presence, was scheduling an appointment. It was then that Scott saw something very curious. Cat was straining to look at the schedule and was even bold enough to ask the receptionist when my appointments were. To Scott's shock and utter amazement, the receptionist willingly supplied this confidential information. Scott turned us around, and we went back into Julie's office, where we confronted her on this flagrant breach of privacy.

We followed Julie back out into the waiting area to speak with Cat and the receptionist, but Cat had already left. The receptionist alone then became the target of the wrath we had just poured out on Julie.

Shortly after this incident I decided that I indeed needed a different counselor. I no longer felt safe at Julie's. Even though the thought of starting over with someone else was overwhelming, the lack of boundaries in the office and what felt like Julie's agenda made my decision to leave relatively easy.

Scott began a search for another Christian counselor. Through his research, he discovered Sonrise Counseling Center (not their actual name). They were a Christian clinic who specialized in cases of extreme trauma. What a find! I can't describe how comforting it was to know that these professionals had a strong grasp of situations like mine. In spite of our enthusiasm, there was still a hurdle to overcome before I could become a client: finances. The services at this clinic were expensive, and we were not just tapped out; we owed everyone else who had helped me up to this point. Our financial black hole continued to expand. It was Scott's family who once again rode to our rescue. His parents and siblings devised a way to cover a majority of the costs we would sustain over the next few years under this oasis of care.

The clinic offered a financial incentive as well. Every session I allowed them to record, they would give me free of charge. These recordings would then be used for teaching purposes in their various seminars. Being desperate and not entirely in the right frame of mind, I agreed to the filming of said appointments.

I soon found myself settling into a routine at the new clinic. My days were filled with twice-weekly individual appointments and one group therapy session. It was through my work with Kathy, my new counselor, that I truly began to discover the source of my volcano of anger connected with Cat and its accompanying fears.

Feeling safe in the hands of those who understood, the flashbacks I had been experiencing since the breakdown intensified. These glimpses gave us insight into what was shaping up as a very frightening past. Most of the upsetting mental images appeared in the early morning hours. With my mind open and body relaxed, I would be stolen away into the realm of a Stephen King novel. Memories came in glimpses that hit every one of my senses: disgusting mixtures of nauseous smells; choking sensations; lights flickering tauntingly around me; mysterious voices in hushed tones; the inability to breathe as if in a cramped, tight space; and invasive sensations. There were always images of blurry people, but one face was consistently clear, a frighteningly familiar face—Cat's face.

My counseling sessions were spent attempting to piece these fragmented visions together. We worked to discover the hidden secrets of my past, the causes of the deep, underlying terrors that had surfaced. I thought my fears were severe before, but as the curtains parted to reveal my past, the fright was overwhelmingly intense. It was not only the fear; the confusion was bewildering. I began to distrust my thoughts and my sense of reality. The horrible scenes that were unfolding were the antithesis of the childhood I remembered ... well, almost. On one hand it seemed impossible that Cat could have been a part of such practices, yet on the other, many disturbing events and experiences now began to make sense. Odd circumstances involving Cat that I had always remembered finally took on significance—places Cat took me, things Cat said, and how Cat sometimes acted. It was difficult accepting the fact that this horrible alternate reality was more than likely a real part of my past no matter how I might fight to deny it.

• • •

SANDY

Approximately six months had come and gone since I had been released from the hospital. I was spending short periods of time at home alone while Scott worked. The emotional pain subsided to the point that, outside of therapy, I was better able to manage on my own. Much of my reasoning skills still functioned at an immature level, but I was making progress. Though we did not own a cell phone, Scott always had his pager handy so I could reach him whenever I needed. At my 911 page he would stop work and run to the nearest pay phone, calling me as quickly as he could. This ability to reach him was a great comfort to me while I was alone yet was difficult for him. I often wrestled with the temptation to use it unnecessarily.

I was home alone one such day when the phone rang.

"Could I please speak to Sandy?" asked the unfamiliar voice.

"Yes, this is Sandy; who is this?"

"This is Bob from AAA News; I just heard Cat speak here in Washington DC and would like to get your side of the story."

I nearly dropped the phone. *Cat is talking about me to people at the nation's capitol? Is this some sick joke?* The confusion that had become a part of my daily life just flew off the charts. "What do you mean you heard Cat speaking in Washington DC? Cat is in Washington?" I asked, completely ignoring the stranger's question and his credentials. My entire body began shaking.

"Yes, Cat is here as a keynote speaker at a convention and just shared a very heart-wrenching account of Cat's relationships being destroyed as a result of a counselor planting ideas of abuse. I want to get your side of this compelling story so we can air it on the national news," Bob continued.

"I don't know what Cat is telling everyone, but I have nothing to say. I just want to be left alone," I managed, sounding reasonably stable in spite of my fearful tremors.

"But think of the impact you could have. By sharing your story, you could help a lot of people in similar circumstances," Bob pressed.

"No, I'm sorry; I have nothing to say," I repeated. "Goodbye," I squeaked out before completely running out of breath as my lungs constricted in panic. I heard Bob's appeal continue as I hung up the phone.

I collapsed on the couch a nervous wreck. My simple life had become so complex and bewildering. *It seems the whole world suddenly knows about me. All I want is to get better and be left alone long enough for that to happen. Is that too much to ask, God? It seems I just get started adjusting to one problem when another pops up. Please help me get my footing here. I feel so tossed about and confused. Lord, what is Cat doing? Why would Cat say such things? I don't understand this. How did this guy get my number anyway? God, please protect us from this unwanted and unsolicited attention!*

I picked up the phone, struggling to resist the urge to page Scott at work. *What could he do anyway? Nothing, but I need to hear his voice*... My shaking hand won out as it dialed the number.

SANDY

We faced many difficult situations in the year following my breakdown, but the most heartbreaking news of all was yet to come.

One afternoon the boys and I sat waiting in the car for Scott to collect payment from a customer. I was feeling particularly good that day, so we were out for a rare family outing.

Listening to the playful sounds of our three sons in the backseat, I found myself reflecting on my own early years. Trying to negotiate the discrepancy between what I thought had been a relatively normal childhood and the nightmare I was remembering, I suddenly found myself needing reassurance that my little guys had been spared from such abuses. Though we'd often talked with them about good and bad touch, I needed to ask again. "Hey, guys, I know I've asked you this before, but has anyone hurt you or touched you in a bad way?" The uncharacteristic silence that followed my simple question unnerved me. Turned in my seat, I could see them looking from one to another, their eyes speaking volumes only they could understand as they carefully considered their answer. My stomach began to knot as I feared what they might say. Then, almost as one, two of them timidly admitted someone had "hurt" them while the third frantically denied it, fearfully repeating that no one had touched him.

I felt as though I had been kicked in the stomach. I couldn't breathe. But regardless of how I felt, I had to be strong for the boys. I did not need to make this difficult situation more painful for them.

I collected a deep breath and calmly asked them who had hurt them. I could see that same fear and apprehension in their eyes as they wrestled with whether or not to tell me. I encouraged them that whatever happened and whoever it was that had harmed them, it was okay to tell me. Soon they, again as one, fearfully confessed the name: Cat.

My head began to swim; my fear of Cat took on a new realism. No longer was this just some strange memory of mine I struggled to comprehend. My own sons were now telling me that this person had harmed them as well. I was faced with the fact that the memories I fought against held more truth than fiction. Regardless of how badly I wanted to deny or refute the images, smells, and sensations I was experiencing, this new information verified my own ordeal.

*Oh God, no!* The wave hit again, full force. I now superimposed the faces of my sons in the violent acts committed against me. Could these same things have happened to them? *Lord, no! How and when could this have happened? Surely there was not opportunity for this same cruelty. How could I have missed this?* Suddenly, a mental light illuminated the signs I had indeed missed. The times the boys would fuss and cry about having to go to Cat's house. I thought they were just bored there. After all, that was the excuse they gave. But boredom had nothing to do with it! I recalled how Cat was always more than happy to take them off my hands for the day and even for the night. What I took as love, generosity, and a helping hand was apparently anything but. How could I have been so blind?

Panic rose in my throat and tears threatened to spill as I considered the horrors the boys might have endured at the hands of this person. Looking into my little guys' eyes I realized I had to pull it together. I knew instinctively that my immediate reaction would have a great and lasting impact on their ability to honestly share and to further deal with their pain, so I fought to restrain myself.

Before going any further, I decided to separate the boys so I could be assured that their accounts would not be influenced by one another. Looking around the car for inspiration, I spotted a few paper plates, clean leftovers from a recent picnic. Inviting one son to the front and suggesting that the other two move apart in the back, I handed each a couple of crayons I'd dug from my purse and one of the paper plates.

"Hey, guys, how about each of you draw me a picture of what happened to you." I tried to keep my voice light and uplifting to hide my own fear and to quell any of theirs. Soon they were all intently involved in their paper plate and crayon snapshots of their painful experiences, while my heart grieved and my mind sought to reconcile the unthinkable.

Scott soon returned to the car. Concerned about the solemn mood that permeated, I quietly filled him in on my recent discovery as we examined the boy's macabre artwork. Scott and I put our own devastated feelings aside while we lovingly spoke to our sons, letting them know how sorry we were that these things had happened to them. Scott promised his young sons that he would protect them from this ever taking place again. He reassured them that they would never be placed in harm's way and he would do whatever it took to keep them safe. But it was if something had been triggered. Each of our sons had shut down and withdrawn within himself as shame and fear quickly took root. Realizing we'd get nowhere at this point, Scott put the car in gear. In a grief-stricken daze, we silently headed for home. As we neared our familiar neighborhood, the boys seemed to gather courage and one by one began to speak, telling a few aspects of abuse they all shared.

Upon entering the house, everyone claimed their spot on the family room furniture as the conversation continued. "Why didn't you tell mommy and me that Cat was hurting you?" Scott coaxed. Unsure about whether or not to open up, they looked at each other for cues. "It's okay," we persuaded. "You can tell us. We won't be angry. We need to know so can protect you."

Reluctantly, they continued. "Cat took us to the gun collection (the one we all knew about) and ... and ... " After a moment's hesitation, they tentatively continued. "Cat said if we ever told anyone about our secret, especially you, Daddy and Mommy, that Cat would shoot and kill all of us!" Scott and I rushed to their sides and enveloped them all as tears filled their innocent eyes. I wanted to hold them tightly so nothing could ever hurt them again. As we stroked their heads, their daddy reassured them that he would never allow Cat to ever harm them again.

From the safe confines of our embrace they hesitantly continued their story, each jumping in, agreeing with and adding to what had been shared.

"Cat took us into the woods," one began.

"... and said they would eat us," another added.

"Who would eat you?" Scott asked.

"The werewolves!" they all three exclaimed emphatically, as though we should know.

We continued to listen as their story unfolded. Cat had taken them out into a wooded area where they were warned of werewolves that roamed about, ready to tear them to pieces if they ever told of their secret.

The power of the secret began to crumble with their disclosure. Their courage grew the more they were able to unburden—that and the fact that we continually reassured them we would keep them safe now that we knew.

Our hearts weighed heavily at the pain and fear our young sons had endured. What kind of parents were we that this abuse had gone on for years right under our noses? In spite of our lessons on good and bad touch, our precious sons had been harmed, and not by some stranger, but by this person whom we often trusted with their young lives. Anything I had gone through paled in comparison to my concern for my sons and the dread contained in these terrifying secrets of theirs.

Our first thoughts were to shield the boys from any further harm and get them all the help they needed. We went into protect mode, doing everything we could to keep our little guys safe. We were grateful that we had cut off our family's contact with Cat as soon as my memories began. We can only speculate that the last few months of separation from this person was what gave them the strength and opportunity to honestly and openly share.

SCOTT

I have never been a violent man, but it took everything within me not to go and beat the living daylights out of Cat for harming my children. Anger did not even begin to explain what I felt. I was beyond furious. Restraining that anger was like holding back a raging bull. I had always been protective of my family and I would do anything to keep them safe. It was only by the grace of God that I did not do something foolish. The evilness of it all was too difficult to even begin to comprehend. *How could someone do those things to small, defenseless, innocent children?* I agonized. I berated myself for not knowing, for not taking better precautions, and for trusting this person. How could Cat have pulled the wool over our eyes for so long? It felt as though I had invited the enemy into our home and given them free reign to wreak havoc and destruction. *God, where were you when all this was happening? Why didn't you stop it? First Sandy, and now my boys! Never again!* I vowed, slamming my fist into the palm of my hand. *Never again!* I would make sure of this. And so began an on-guard, vigilant stance—a cynical, untrusting posture I would hold for years, one that would be difficult to eventually release.

Fearing I could no longer trust God to protect my family, I took on this responsibility myself and swore to do whatever it took to ensure the safety of my family. My mind could not reconcile how something so terrible could happen to a child of God. It had always been my belief that God would never allow something this traumatic to happen to my family. The fact that it did dealt a devastating blow to my trust and sense of security. I did not know if my staggering faith could ever recover.

SANDY

By this time our finances were decimated and we were considered to be at the poverty level, qualifying for government aid. I called a counseling agency on our list of state providers in hopes of getting the boys immediate help. As I explained our situation to one of the counselors, I was met with an unexpected response. "We could make an appointment for your sons, but you need to call the police first."

"The police? Why do I need to call the police?" I asked. "It isn't like this just happened; they haven't seen this person for several months now." (Soon after my discharge from the hospital, we pulled back from all family and family friends, as we were not certain whom we could trust.) I was so focused on helping the boys that I had not considered involving the police. I just wanted God to wrap our little family in a blanket of love and protect us from further harm. I did not want this to turn into a big legal or bureaucratic ordeal. For the boys' sake, I wanted their healing process to be as quiet and calm as possible.

"If you don't call and make a report, we will be required to. If you do not initiate the call yourself, Child Protective Services might assume you bear some responsibility."

I thanked the counselor and said I would call back once we involved the authorities. I feared for the boys. They were terrified to share what little they had with us; I could not imagine what it would be like to have to say those things to the police.

I shared this new information with Scott, and we prayed together before making the dreaded call.

Two officers entered our house within the hour. Their presence and demeanor as they stood in their imposing uniforms was intimidating. The boys sat on the couch in a silent row, their eyes full of fear as the policemen got right down to business, wanting to know the facts. As I had suspected, our little guys did not say a word. It had taken so much courage for them to tell us, their own mommy and daddy. How anyone expected them to be able to tell businesslike strangers, especially in such commanding attire, was beyond me.

Unable to get the information they needed, the officers made arrangements for us to visit the station the following day. The boys did not want to go, but we did our best to assure them they would be okay.

The experience at the station was no better. The officers at that time were not trained to work with children as they are today. The boys were taken from us, separated, placed in individual rooms, and seated at large conference tables. The special toys and blankets I brought along offered them no comfort in such an overwhelming and scary environment. In spite of the officers' best efforts, our three sons had shut down and refused to speak. With nothing from which to work, their hands were tied. They filed a report and told us there was nothing more they could do until the boys were willing to offer further evidence. They then insisted we get a restraining order against Cat, which we did the very next day.

Though it was frustrating that Cat was not to be prosecuted, we were grateful that the boys would not be testifying against the person they feared would shoot them. We'd all had enough trauma for now.

After learning of the boys' abuse, Sonrise Counseling Center worked with Scott's family and created a way for our young sons to get help from the same counselor I was seeing. The continuity in the therapy was helpful for us all. However, in spite of the help, life only grew more difficult. The boys were too young to understand what they had been through, let alone how they felt about it all. Sometimes they lashed out in anger, while at others they withdrew in fear. Parenting became extremely difficult, especially since I was not in a solid place myself. Much of the difficulty, unfortunately, fell on Scott's shoulders. Though I was not emotionally strong enough to always hand out appropriate disciplines, I did provide our sons with love and understanding.

Those first few months were filled with intensity and turmoil as we all sought to deal with this devastating blow. The overwhelming emotions proved to be too much for one of our little guys and like me, he too required hospitalization. Leaving him in the hands of the hospital staff at such a young age and in so much emotional pain nearly tore our hearts in two. But we were not able to provide him with all he needed to safely work through his trauma. This was one of the darkest hours in our lives.

Because Scott had reached his limit and could not handle going through that process a second time, the responsibility for making the hospital arrangements fell on me. Hospitalizing me had been very difficult for him. He always tried to be so strong for us, but I was concerned about all the feelings he was internalizing. I was not sure how much longer he could continue at this pace. He never had an opportunity to let his guard down. He struggled with guilt and regret at not being able to protect us, but I assured him it was not his fault. Scott was in a tremendous amount of pain, and this decision to hospitalize our son was eating him alive. Watching our three innocent little guys dealing with their pain was the most difficult experience of all.

SANDY

"Honey, come quick, you will not believe this!" I called for Scott as I sat aghast in front of the TV watching the local news one evening. He came running in just as the anchor woman cut to the reporter standing next to none other than Cat, who looked completely distraught. Cat carried on about being the victim of false accusations and that our family had been divided as a result. The tears even looked genuine. Someone unaware of our situation would have felt a great deal of compassion and empathy. In spite of our attempts to keep this a private matter, Cat continued to seek the spotlight.

Even the local paper picked up Cat's story, reporting a variety of distorted facts over several articles. Bob, from AAA News, and other national reporters continued to call, pressuring me to tell my side of this apparently juicy, must-have story. We just wanted to be left alone. We needed time and space to absorb and work through all the bewildering events that left us reeling.

# SURVIVAL SKILL #1

# *Accept the Reality of What Is*

> What "should be" doesn't exist; it never did. But the good news is, what "could be" has yet to be written.
>
> Author unknown

SCOTT AND SANDY

At this point in time, our family lived in a constant state of upheaval. Each day was filled with chaos and uncertainty. We barely kept our heads above water. This was, without a doubt, one of the most difficult periods in our family's life. We were completely unprepared when disaster hit. But then again, how does one prepare for an unexpected tragedy? It soon became obvious that we lacked the necessary life tools to effectively deal with our sudden and unforeseen struggles. So we did what came naturally: we resented and fought against our situation.

After years of struggling, the futility of this battle became clear. Resisting and combating these unwelcome struggles did nothing to improve or change our situation. Rather, it trapped us within them. We were not gaining any ground; we were struggling with the same problems day in and day out. We had one major goal: survive the day. This constant struggle to endure was getting old, and we soon grew tired of just surviving. To be quite honest, we didn't know how much longer we could continue to live in this survival mode. Certainly there had to be more to life than this. We were desperately ready for change. Fortunately, change was possible; but we first needed a critical life tool in order to make this change a reality.

It was at this point that we discovered our first Survival Skill: *Accept the Reality of What Is.*

A powerful principle was at work, one that could no longer be ignored: we could not change that which we did not first *accept.* Only through *acceptance* could we escape our survival posture and begin to take the necessary steps that would improve our situation.

Before we could practice the skill of accepting, we first needed to understand the concept of acceptance. What stood between us and the freedom acceptance offered was our distorted view of this concept. Up to this point, we mistakenly believed that to accept what happened to us and the difficult conditions that followed would mean that we were conceding that what had happened was okay and therefore acceptable. This we would not do. The horrible offenses committed against our family were not okay.

Acceptance is never to be confused with excusing
or tolerating uncomfortable, inappropriate, or
even abusive behaviors or conditions.

As we discovered the truth about acceptance, we came to realize that we did not have to agree with our circumstances in order to accept them. Accepting what happened did not justify what happened. We did not have to give up hope that things would change and therefore, settle for a defeated and miserable life. Furthermore, we did not have to tolerate uncomfortable, inappropriate, or even abusive behavior. We could set boundaries. And we did.

Acceptance simply acknowledged that though what happened to us shouldn't have, the truth was it did. Acceptance merely required that we be honest with ourselves about the way things were rather than obsessing about how we felt they should or should not be. No more. No less.

*Acceptance* is simply being honest with yourself
about the way things are. No more. No less.

With acceptance understood, the next step was to make the choice to accept all that we had previously been resisting. The process of acceptance was as simple as making the choice to accept. This did not make acceptance easy, but it did make it doable.

By making the shift into accepting the reality of *what is* in our lives, we took the first major step toward changing our painful circumstances. No longer would we be limited to our reactions. We could now be proactive. For the first time in a long while, positive change began to occur and life began to feel hopeful again. We felt free from the constraints of our resistance, and we were finally able to let down our battle mentality and relax.

Another benefit of accepting was that it allowed us to operate in the realm of what was actual and true. Conversely, when we resisted our circumstances as though they shouldn't be, we operated in the realm of distortion, diversions, and falsehoods. Obsessing about how things should be and what shouldn't have happened merely threw us into a fantasy world. It wasn't true. What was true was that what should have happened didn't happen, and what shouldn't have happened did happen. The only way we were going to move forward and affect positive change in our lives was by dealing with this truth-based reality.

Though acceptance has, at times, been difficult for us and has required hard work, the effort invested has been worth it.

Breaking free from resisting the reality of *what is* has literally changed our lives for the better.

Resisting the acceptance of *what is* routinely shows up in three basic forms:

- *Blind Avoidance*–A choice, at either a conscious or an unconscious level, to not know what needs to be known.
- *Demanding "Shoulds"*–Insistent expectations of how one feels things should or should not be.
- *Non-Accepting "Why*s"–"Why" questions that are asked not for the purpose of understanding, but as a way to protest one's frustration and disagreement with *what is.*

We have personally struggled with each of these areas at various times along our journey. Let us share with you how they showed up for us:

SANDY

I had not realized it, but the first twenty-eight years of my life were spent in an unintentional *blind avoidance* of my past. Distancing myself from my previous traumatic events by compartmentalizing and storing them far away from my conscious awareness (as though they never happened) was a perfect coping skill. Though this action was unintentional and completely subconscious, it was a blessing that proved to keep me mentally intact and emotionally protected enough to live a normal life. However, my neatly packaged boxes storing painful memories eventually became a liability to my family and myself, as they kept me from vital knowledge, knowledge that could have kept my family safe.

Once the hurricane of my breakdown tore apart my carefully constructed storeroom of memories, I was given the opportunity to look at that which I had tucked away: the reality, or truth, of my frightening past. When I opened my eyes to what had always existed, I quickly took proactive steps to protect those I loved from the same dangers I had been exposed to as a young child. I no longer allowed *blind avoidance* a place in my life. As I regained my mental and emotional health, I chose to live in the truth, no matter how ugly or scary it appeared. I must admit, at times, living with this choice has been difficult. But now I can live with my eyes wide open, realizing that God will give me the grace to handle whatever I need to know and when necessary, the power to act.

SCOTT

At the time of Sandy's breakdown, I saw my hopes and dreams crumble down around me. Being a planner and a doer, I had goals and desires for myself and my family and worked diligently to make them a reality. However, when I temporarily lost my wife and everything for which I had sacrificed and toiled, it rocked my world. I could not accept the fact that my aspirations and my wife were suddenly taken away from me. Or, as I later discovered, I wouldn't accept it.

Those who hear our story would probably agree that I had a good case to argue. The abuses and injustices shouldn't have happened. But the cold, hard truth of the matter was that they did. I lost my dreams, possessions, my wife (temporarily), and the ability to protect my sons. Sandy and our boys were traumatized and no amount of "shoulds" or "should nots" on my part was ever going to change this painful yet true reality. No matter how passionately I held to what should or should not have happened, it did not change the reality of what did, in fact, happen. What it did change, however, was me, and I don't mean in a positive way. Fighting against how things were only compounded my problems, frustrated me, and caused me to me to feel helpless and hopeless. I found myself becoming increasingly cynical about life and overly vigilant to protect those I loved. Misery and frustration were constant companions.

It soon became clear to me that my resistance was one of those areas that fell into the "fix me" category about which God had earlier spoken, and rightly so. My preoccupation with how things should be threw me into a state of delusion. Though focusing on what should be appeared to be the logical course of action, it was actually illogical; what should be was irrelevant, because it wasn't. As long as I operated in this place of un-reality, I was literally powerless to do anything to tangibly change or improve our situation.

A prime example was my experience with the hospital finance manager who threatened to carry Sandy to the curb if she didn't receive my money. I was so infuriated by this woman's insensitivity and how I felt she should've handled our situation that it locked up my brain, preventing me from constructing a creative strategy for funding Sandy's stay. How this administrator should have handled our situation did not change my reality: I needed to generate six thousand dollars in two days' time. By accepting rather than resisting my dilemma, I was able to focus on the real issue: my need to pay the bill. Without the distraction of my inner battle, I was able to find resourceful and even inspired options for solving the actual problem.

SANDY

Though Scott and I both often struggled to understand the *why* of our circumstances, I went through a period of time where I became obsessed with a preoccupation of asking why. "*Why* did Cat do such hurtful things to my sons and me?" "*Why* did God allow these traumatic events to happen?" "*Why* isn't he answering our prayers?" "*Why* is our life continually getting worse instead of getting better?" "*Why* do our boys have to suffer?"

Within that first year, my ailing grandmother passed away. I desperately wanted to attend her funeral, yet, knowing Cat would be present, I decided not to go. On top of everything else, I had missed out on the last few months of my grandmother's life and now her funeral. "Why couldn't this have all come out after Grandma died?" was another agonizing frustration and a difficult *why* to accept.

At first, asking why seemed the logical thing to do. After all, it is good to understand one's plight through healthy reflection. This affords one the ability to learn from previous mistakes and failures. Early on, asking why provided me a form of comfort, a reprieve from my distress. However, I soon realized that my continual *why* questions were actually another form of avoidance and an expression of my own resistance. My curious *whys* had digressed into *non-accepting whys.* A *non-accepting why* is a term we use to define those questions whose answers serve no real purpose in moving us forward. They are like the proverbial squeaky hamster wheel going round and round a topic while making no discernable progress—only a lot of distracting noise. We can also draw a comparison to the angry child who does not like the answer he receives. In his defiance he repeatedly asks "why" as an expression of his contention, not to truly seek an answer.

My *non-accepting whys* thwarted my progress and kept me stuck. The clarity and understanding that my mind so desperately sought turned to confusion. I became stuck in an endless loop of what ifs and infinite possibilities. My mental attic became so cluttered that it was next to impossible to navigate.

The truth was my family and I were victimized. However, in order to move beyond my experiences and not continue to live as a victim, I first needed to stop asking why and accept the painful reality that what happened, happened. With God's help, I worked through the loss and enough of the confusion that I was finally able to move into acceptance. I still didn't have the answers I desired, but I was able to come to the point that those questions no longer haunted me. Breaking free from the bonds of *why* gave me momentum I required in order to move forward.

# IT'S YOUR TURN

SCOTT AND SANDY

Now it's your turn. Consider these questions:

- Are you struggling to accept your current circumstances as they are?
- What about your past experiences? In what ways might you be resisting them (blind avoidance, demanding shoulds, non-accepting whys)?
- Has your resistance improved your situation or worsened it?
- What has your resistance cost you: (peace, growth, hope, relationships)?

Maybe it's time for you to stop resisting your circumstances and accept (not give in to) the reality of *what is* in your life. Accept the fact that regardless of how things should be, they are what they are.

We understand how difficult *accepting* your present and past experiences may be for you. The idea of doing so may even stir up deep feelings of anger. That is okay. This process is meant to stretch you. You will be using new spiritual and emotional muscles you might not have used before. Like any new exercise, you might experience some discomfort at first. Don't worry; this is natural.

If you are still experiencing some reluctance, you might find the following steps helpful:

## *Clear Out Your Misconceptions*

Begin by eliminating any misconceptions that you have regarding acceptance. Look at the following list and check off any that relate to you.

Common misconceptions about *Acceptance:*

To accept my current circumstances as they are would mean:

- ☐ I am giving up.
- ☐ I am giving in to something I feel compelled to fight.
- ☐ The bad things that happen to me are okay and acceptable.
- ☐ I have to ignore and stuff my feelings.
- ☐ I don't care anymore.
- ☐ I will have to tolerate inappropriate behavior.
- ☐ Nothing will ever change.
- ☐ I will become swallowed up in the trauma and pain of the present and past.

Remember, accepting the reality of your painful experiences does not require you to agree with them, understand them, or even like them. It doesn't make the wrong things right. It does not mean that you are giving up. Acceptance is not to be confused with excusing or tolerating uncomfortable, inappropriate, or even abusive behaviors or conditions. It simply acknowledges that such behaviors may exist in your life. In a nutshell, acceptance is simply being honest with yourself about the way things *are.* No more. No less.

From this place of acceptance, you can now begin to pursue and implement healthy actions that will improve and change your situation.

## *Choose Acceptance*

Acceptance is as simple (though not necessarily as easy) as making the choice to accept. You can choose to accept the reality of your circumstances, or you can choose to resist them. The choice is yours. No one can make it for you. Just remember, you will not be able to fully change that which you do not first accept.

## *Open Your Eyes*

Next, open your eyes and see what is really there. You may not have experienced traumatic incidents causing you to block out what you need to know, but you may still be ignoring the reality of *what is.*

Years ago our dog, Muffy, a Doxa-Cocka-Whatever mix, used to play her own version of Hide and Seek. If we called her name and she did not want to come, she would freeze and avoid eye contact. She believed that as long as she did not see us we could not see her; therefore, she was free of our demand.

Many people implement this same practice when they do not want to acknowledge or deal with something. As long as they do not look at or think about their problem, it will just disappear. This magical thinking can cause devastating effects. The reality is: what you do not know, accept, or acknowledge can indeed hurt you and those around you as well. Problems and responsibilities do not just go away by ignoring them. Ignoring them actually increases the likelihood that you will remain tethered to them.

What I do not know, accept, or acknowledge can
indeed hurt me and those around me as well.

What is it in your life that you have chosen not to see? How has doing so hindered or even hurt you and others around you? Without getting down on yourself, we encourage you to look at whatever it is that you need to see. Be fully honest and transparent with yourself. Ask God to give you the strength and ability to see what needs to be seen. If you need assistance, seek out someone you trust to help you sort things through, or pursue professional counseling or coaching.

## *Let Go of Your Demanding Shoulds*

SCOTT

Are you a strong *should-er?* Do you adhere fiercely to how you believe things and others *should* be? When things go badly, do you have the tendency to resist them by obsessing about how they should be? If so, welcome to the Should-ers Club, of which I am a card-carrying member. There is something deeply ingrained in each of us that can strongly react against the things in our lives that aren't the way we feel they should be. Though this is a natural reaction, it is not necessarily a healthy one. Remember, no amount of *should* will change the way things *are.* As someone once said: "What should be doesn't exist; it never did; there only is what is."

Are you suffering from Should-ers Heart?

- ☐ *Shoulds* and *should nots* preoccupy my thoughts and control my attitude and emotions.
- ☐ I feel overwhelmed and anxious whenever I discuss or think about my circumstances.
- ☐ I am exhausted and fatigued from battling against my situation.
- ☐ I feel depressed and hopeless about my life.
- ☐ I have become angry and embittered over my experiences and conditions.
- ☐ I am unable to rest, relax, or disengage my mind from how I believe things and others *should be.*
- ☐ I have become stuck in the very thing I have been resisting.
- ☐ It would be difficult to let go of how I believe others and things *should be.*

SCOTT AND SANDY

If the answer to any of these questions is yes, then you may be suffering from Should-ers Heart. Should-ers Heart is a phrase we coined as a spinoff from an older term that came to be used during the Civil War, called Soldiers Heart Syndrome. This reference described soldiers who had fought too hard and for too long. These brave men of old were not able to disengage from a battle mentality. As a result, their mind and body were in a constant state of war and they were unable to detach from the battle, even when off the battlefield.

Though you may not be in a physical battle, you may have waged an inner war of shoulds for so long that you find yourself unable to disengage. If so, it is time to stop fighting and pull away from the battlefield of your shoulds. Take a much-needed rest and gain a fresh perspective. Unhook the circumstances and people in your life from the stranglehold of your shoulds. Let go of these shoulds and accept the fact that it is what it is ... for now. Just for now.

We are not saying that all shoulds must be eliminated. There are legitimate shoulds. For example, when you get married and promise to be true to each other, neither of you should be unfaithful. You should be able to trust each other. However, sadly, this expectation does not guarantee that both of you will remain faithful. If you are the unfortunate casualty of an unfaithful relationship, no amount of "it shouldn't have happened" will remove the painful fact that it did. There are other, more effective ways to help protect your relationship from the ravages of infidelity as opposed to merely pouring your energies into your shoulds.

## *Replace Your Whys with How and What*

Asking "why" comes so naturally, doesn't it? Whenever we do not agree with something, our default is often to protest it by asking why. Perhaps that's because asking, or even demanding, why makes us feel as though we have some level of control. Maybe we believe that if we can understand our trials it will somehow make accepting them easier. There might be some truth to that line of thinking. However, waiting to accept our situation until we fully understand it can leave us in limbo a very long time, and we'll experience much grief in the interim. The difficult truth is: we may never understand the *why* of some of our experiences, this side of eternity.

Asking why can easily become another form of resistance to accepting what really is. Whereas shoulds are a more aggressive form of resistance, our whys tend to be more of a passive means of avoidance. When you become stuck in *non-accepting whys,* you are really saying, "I will accept what is happening to me as long as I can understand and agree with it." The truth is that regardless of what you know or agree with, whatever happened still happened and nothing can change that fact.

Let us make a simple suggestion that we have found particularly helpful in eliminating our *non-accepting whys* from our verbal and mental vocabulary. When you find yourself bogged down in your whys, rephrase your why questions into *how* and *what* solutions. Yes, we said solutions. *How* and *what* questions are forward moving and empowering. They are action oriented and will help you navigate your way through your problematic situations.

For example, the next time you catch yourself repeating "Why is this happening to me?" replace your non-accepting question with any of the following:

- *How* is my need to know why this is happening serving me? Is it in any way helping me accept my circumstances?
- *What* expectations can I let go of that might help me more fully accept my situation?

- *What* can I discover or learn about myself or God as a result of my circumstances?
- After accepting the reality of my situation, *what* steps can I take to improve or change it?
- *How* may God be using my current circumstances as a catalyst for my growth or re-direction?

### *Grieve Over the Losses That Have Occurred*

Don't be surprised if painful emotions present themselves as you move out of resistance and into acceptance. It is common for uncomfortable feelings to surface once you begin to accept the losses, pain, frustrations, and injustices you have resisted for so long. Once we stopped resisting our reality and moved into the *acceptance of what is,* we experienced a rollercoaster of emotions. On the one hand, we felt liberated from the demands of our shoulds and released from our obsession with our whys, while on the other, we experienced a tremendous amount of grief, loss, sadness, depression, and even anger.

When this natural grieving process presents itself, allow it to run its course. Common stages in the grieving process are: shock, anger, depression, sadness, and finally, letting go and moving on. Permit yourself to feel these uncomfortable feelings. They won't last forever. They are an essential part of the healing process. Allowing yourself to process these emotions will help you to put closure to your painful experiences and enable you to move forward.

## CONCLUSION

Life will always have obstacles—catalysts, if you will. These opportunities are intended to initiate growth and positive changes. But when we resist the catalyst—*what is*—we become stuck in an endless loop of whys, trapped and embittered by our shoulds, or we sit in denial, closing our eyes like a terrified child and hoping it will all just magically disappear.

You can choose how you will handle your catalyst. Will you make the most of this opportunity and leverage it to your advantage, using it as a tool to help you grow and move into what God has for you? Or will you resist it and risk becoming stuck and embittered?

We encourage you to accept whatever trials are presenting themselves in your life. It is only after you accept the way things truly are that you free yourself up to make necessary or desired improvements and changes.

# *Unseen Enemies*

SCOTT

"Lord, we aren't sure what is happening, and we don't even really know how to pray about it. Based on what we have recently learned, we ask you to place a hedge of protection around our family and our home. Please send angels to stand guard over us."

With that simple prayer, we dove headfirst into an unfamiliar battle—a war we did not entirely understand, against an enemy we could not see.

"In the name of Jesus Christ and by his authority we command every evil presence to leave us. We renounce and sever any and all connections with you. Through Christ's work on the cross, we command that you leave our family now," I addressed the unseen foe, taking my first offensive stand in this decidedly spiritual battle for my family.

As if on cue, one of our sons, who had asked to sleep on the floor of our bedroom that evening (this was becoming a common occurrence), was abruptly awakened from his sound sleep by a searing pain. His bloodcurdling screams sent us off the living room couch and running to our bedroom in record time.

"Something is chewing on my stomach! It's chewing on my stomach," he cried out in extreme pain.

We scanned his body, looking for the source of his agony. Our child was clearly awake; this was not a nightmare. His pain was real, yet he had no fever or outward signs of sickness or trauma. Still, we could not ignore his own description of something "chewing" on his stomach. In the same moment, Sandy and I were hit with an identical thought: *Is this somehow connected with our prayer?* Looking at each other with a knowing gaze, Sandy said what we both were thinking: "We should lay our hands on him and pray."

Quickly placing our hands on his abdomen, I repeated my previous command. This time I delivered it with the authority I held as the father and protector of my son. No one, seen or unseen, was going to hurt him again! "In the name of Jesus, leave my son *now!*" Instantly, his screaming stopped. Not even a trace of the excruciating pain remained. Our son looked up at us with the same incredulous expression we both carried. Scooping him into our arms, we cradled him and calmed his fears. Sandy thanked God for freeing our son from the grasp of this evil presence while she soothed his fears. I sat there struggling to take in all that had just happened.

Finally feeling comforted, our son looked to us for an explanation. "Mom and Dad, it felt like there were teeth biting my stomach and chewing it up; it hurt so bad! What was it?"

Hard pressed to understand this strange encounter ourselves, we did our best to explain it to our confused and frightened son. "We don't understand either, but we do know this: Jesus took your pain away. He loves you, and he is always with you. If something like this ever happens again, just ask him to help you and he will. You don't have to be afraid," I explained, thankful that God had intervened on my young boy's behalf.

SANDY

It was as though a portal to hell itself opened into our home, unleashing its full fury upon us; at least, that is how it felt. It all began within a month after I was discharged from the hospital. The flashbacks I experienced grew more troublesome. At first, we wondered if our family was just being paranoid. The five of us began seeing mysterious shadows and hearing strange, unusual noises. Even our dog seemed to be affected. We also had the distinct feeling we were being watched.

The more I uncovered about my past, the more intense the hellish torment grew. Our boys especially were targeted by these attacks. The children began experiencing night terrors and a myriad of other supernatural encounters.

Another of our sons became convinced that his daddy and brothers were lying in wait to ambush him with knives. It wasn't until I found him hiding, fearing for his life, that Scott and I were able to help him. Through the authority of Christ, we broke the power that this malicious villain held over our son's innocent mind. As this malevolent spirit left, Scott and I both felt the icy presence shoot right through us, literally taking our breath away.

During this time, one of our sons also began sleepwalking, often attempting to get out of the house while the rest of us slept. Scott installed special alarms to warn us when a door or window was being opened. Even with the extra precautions in place, he developed the habit of waking up several times during the night to check on the boys.

It was uncomfortable sharing these bizarre experiences with friends. Some thought we had gone off the deep end, while others pulled back in fear, as though our spiritual troubles were somehow contagious. Whatever their reason, the end result was the same: we felt isolated and alone. In a sense, we really couldn't blame our friends. If we hadn't actually experienced these things firsthand, we too would have had trouble believing a story such as ours. The unseen enemies involved in our struggle were difficult to understand if you weren't actively engaged in the battle.

As we were lonely, wounded, and especially vulnerable, God, in his perfect timing, gave us the gift of two very special families. These precious friends not only provided us with personal support and understanding, but they were also spiritual counselors who helped us through this difficult time.

It wasn't long before God also led us to a church that grasped the magnitude of our struggle. Its members accepted, supported, and encouraged us in a way we had never before experienced. They not only became our respite from the battle but fellow soldiers in the trenches as well. It was comforting to finally have a church home after a year of isolation.

SCOTT

The first Sunday we visited this powerful little community of believers, we knew we had found a church home. At the end of the service Pastor Douglas approached me, enthusiastically shaking my hand. He asked if we could sit and chat for a few minutes, so we each took a chair from the back row. After a warm welcome and some introductory small talk he asked, "So what brings you to our little church?" His simple question touched a painful nerve. I was looking out the window, considering my answer, when my mind transported me back one year in time, two months after Sandy's release from the hospital …

> Pastor Lou had called, inviting me to coffee. As I walked into Denny's, I quickly spotted him in one of the corner booths. We shook hands and exchanged pleasantries. My initial excitement began to fade, overshadowed by a sudden uneasy feeling. Something wasn't right; I just couldn't put my finger on it.
>
> I considered Lou a friend. He and I had met regularly for some time. He offered his support and lent an ear when I needed to talk. He was keenly aware of our situation from

the very beginning and fully supported us, in spite of the complexities of our problems. His encouragement had been an anchor in my suddenly tumultuous life, but his demeanor today was different. He seemed cold and detached, not the kind, supportive friend I had come to know and appreciate.

"Scott," Pastor Lou began, "I'm going to get right to the point. I'm not sure how I really feel about Sandy's situation."

*What? Where is this coming from?*

"If therapy was really working for Sandy," he continued, "she would be better by now, or at least much more improved."

*Wait a minute! Are we on trial here?* I could feel the hair on the back of my neck stand at attention as I readied to defend my wife.

Before I could even respond, he continued. "The people in church are beginning to talk. They are concerned because they see no improvement in Sandy when they deliver meals. Some are even beginning to wonder if this is all just an act to get attention."

Now I was angry! *No one came to us with any concerns whenever they delivered dinner. Besides, we didn't even ask for help. You guys are the ones who offered.*

Once again, before I could speak my mind and counter the implied accusation, he went on. "Scott, the bottom line is, people are getting tired of helping, and they want to see improvements."

Clenching my fists, I fought to maintain my composure and not react defensively. "Wait a minute, Lou; Sandy *is* improving! Yes, the process is slow, but the doctors said it would be. She's working hard in therapy. What more do you want her to do? Besides, you know all of this."

As though I had not spoken at all, he continued. "We had to discipline one in our congregation. The wife claimed to have chronic fatigue syndrome, and it didn't appear she was get-

> ting help for her problem. As a matter of fact, she seemed to be taking advantage of the church's generosity."
>
> I had to take a deep breath to calm myself; my friend's insinuations left my mind reeling. I was both angry and dumbfounded. This sudden change was so incongruent with everything up to this point.
>
> His next statement made it all clear.
>
> "If you feel it necessary to find another church, we would certainly understand. We don't want you and Sandy to feel obligated to stay here."
>
> *So that's what he is getting at; he wants us to leave.* The rejection hit me full force as I realized we were no longer welcome in our church home. In this stunned condition, words eluded me as I looked into the face of the man I had considered my friend.

A fly buzzed my ear, jolting me back to the present. Pastor Douglas sat patiently awaiting my reply. If he wondered what I was thinking and why it took me so long to answer, he never asked. I cleared my throat as I tried to reorient myself. "Well, we have been through some very difficult times. We are looking for a church that understands the battle we have been fighting, and yours came highly recommended." I was still a bit gun-shy from our previous church experience, but I silently prayed God would give this pastor the understanding and wisdom he would need to help us. I also hoped that we would not overwhelm this church and experience the same rejection. As our conversation continued, Pastor Douglas and I were soon joined by his wife, Reina, and Sandy. The four of us enjoyed a short conversation before we left. Sandy and I gathered the boys and walked hand in hand to our car, smiling for the first time in a long while.

SANDY

In spite of God's blessings, as the weeks progressed, our daily struggles continued. Our son who had been hospitalized qualified for specialized in-home treatment through the state. Each week, two social workers came into our home to help us parent our troubled sons. Their visits were a blessing to me in particular, as I was having a difficult time setting limitations with the boys. With the overall confusion and fragmented thinking I suffered since the breakdown, my sons were getting away with far more than they should. After all they had been through, they needed the safety and the comfort of boundaries and limitations now more than ever.

In spite of the further evidence unearthed through the boys' therapy, we never did go back to the police to pursue a conviction for Cat. Our sons were having a difficult enough time coping; we did not want to traumatize them further by forcing them to face their abuser. Having already warned family members with children about the boys' situation with Cat, we were fairly confident that no other children were in harm's way.

We did, however, take an additional step to ensure our safety. At the suggestion of several counselors, I wrote a letter to my entire extended family and close family friends. In this letter, I explained that my family and I needed time alone to heal. I thanked them for their concern but asked that they give us as much space as we needed to work through our pain. I included a third-party contact number they could use for emergencies.

With all the strange things we were experiencing, we did not know if Cat was the only unsafe person in our life. Our world was so upside down we didn't know who we could trust. However, there were a few family members we believed posed no threat. We discreetly maintained minimal contact with these select few. Naturally, there were some who were uncomfortable with the family rift my situation created. These individuals could not stay completely away. Finding family members and family friends on my doorstep, demanding that I work out my differences with Cat, were situations that were quite difficult to navigate. They did not have the full story, and we were not yet willing to share it. These encounters often left me fearful to answer the door, worrying what confrontation might be waiting for me on the other side.

SCOTT

We returned home at twilight one evening and opened the back door to check on our dog. The sun, suspended in the western sky, set the yard in an unusual eerie glow, but I was too distracted to notice. At my call, Tiny came running, and I bent to scratch behind his floppy ears. Not one to remain in one place for long, our mutt ran into the house to greet his boys. As I stood up, my eyes landed on a frightening sight. Through the strange haze, I saw a circle of dead birds, all missing their heads. Our private little grassy patch had become a macabre graveyard. Beyond the missing heads, I could not dismiss the fact that the birds appeared to be placed in a near-perfect circle.

I heard a gasp behind me. "Who would have done such a cruel thing?" Sandy asked as she crowded me in the doorway, appalled at the carnage.

"I don't know, but some *one* had to have done it," I answered. Unlike our previous strange, supernatural encounters, the culprit here certainly had to be one of flesh and blood. *Is this some sort of witchcraft or voodoo? Is someone sending us a cryptic message?* My mind considered the worst.

In spite of my suspicions, I resisted the urge to jump to any conclusions. The boys, who were now drawn to the glass door as well, stared curiously at the headless state of the sparrows. I could see their apprehension through their fascination as they wondered how the birds met such a fate. Sandy pulled the drapes and took the boys into the other room in spite of their objections. She kept them sufficiently distracted while I inspected the yard in search of a reasonable answer.

I checked the gate for evidence of tampering and looked for unfamiliar footprints in the surrounding loose dirt. Standing on my toes, I peered over the block fence into the adjoining park, searching for both the signs of an intruder and the missing heads. I needed to find something that would help me fit the pieces of this bizarre puzzle together. Yet I found nothing.

At this point I debated whether I should call the police. *What would I tell them?* I highly doubted that six dead birds would be high on their priority list of crimes. Deciding against the idea, I set about to clear the gruesome scene. With trash bag in hand, I bent down and carefully picked up the first innocent victim by its fragile legs. As I inspected the mortal wound, my thoughts couldn't help but turn to the boys. They had experienced and witnessed so many frightening things lately. What kind of an impact was all of this going to have on their young, impressionable lives?

Shaking off my concerns, I hurried to continue the cleanup before the sun went down. Tiny, our neurotic Springer-Spaniel mix, followed me around the yard. He sniffed knowingly at each bird as though he held the answers I sought. I looked deeply into his big, brown eyes, willing him to somehow tell me what he knew.

Just then, a little sparrow landed in the yard, instantly catching the dog's eye. What he did next completely surprised me. He hunkered down and stalked the unsuspecting bird with the stealth of a lion. Then, with a swiftness I'd never before witnessed from this dog, he jumped through the air and pounced on the poor, defenseless bird. "No, Tiny!" I shouted as I ran toward him in an attempt to rescue the bird, but it was too late. Tiny was quick.

Although disgusted by yet another of Tiny's growing list of unacceptable behaviors, I couldn't help but let out a huge sigh of relief. The realization hit me that the gruesome scene was not the result of some heinous evil after all. Sharing my findings with Sandy, she scolded Tiny for his despicable act but felt a deep sense of relief as well.

Still, the fact that all the birds had been placed in such a neat circle did not escape my attention. Not wanting to say anything that might ruin the sense of relief that my family experienced, I kept my concern to myself.

• • •

SCOTT

"Hello?" I said, after reaching for the phone.

"Scott, this is Kathy, I'm calling to let you know we had a break-in at the center last night."

"Is everything all right? Was anyone hurt?" I inquired. The situation was obviously important, but I wondered why Sandy's counselor was sharing it with me.

"Thankfully, everyone is okay. No one was here when it happened, but it is rather strange. The police had us do a thorough search of the office, and the only things missing are the video tapes we made of Sandy's sessions."

"You've got to be kidding! No other tapes were taken?"

"No, only the videos we recorded of Sandy. I need to let you know that the staff shared their concern for your family during our prayer time this morning. Based on what you guys have experienced, and now with this new development, we feel it would be a good idea for you to take extra precautions to keep your family safe."

Hanging up the phone, I tried to assimilate this new turn of events. *How strange that Sandy's recordings were the only things stolen. Who would stand to gain by stealing Sandy's therapy videos? What information on those tapes could be so valuable that someone would risk breaking in to steal them?* Though I had my ideas, I kept them to myself. I made a mental note to obtain a more protective breed of dog.

Although I did not want to scare her, I decided that I had better tell Sandy about the break-in. She would find out sooner or later; I thought it would be better coming from me.

"Oh no! My tapes were stolen? Why were only my tapes taken? Who would want them, anyway?" Sandy cried out. "I don't want some stranger watching videos of me pouring my heart out and sharing my deepest and darkest fears. I should never have agreed to allow the center to record my sessions in the first place!" Sandy's self-reprimand didn't last long, as her frustration was eclipsed by panic. "What does this mean for our family? You know how scary some of the stuff I'm remembering is. If those memories are really true, what does that mean for us now? This can't be coincidental, not with all the other strange things that have been happening. Could Cat be behind this?"

Sandy paused for a moment. I heard her catch her breath as she asked, "Scott, are we safe?"

*Are we safe?* A chill crawled up my spine as I absorbed the frightening gravity of her question.

I tried to reassure Sandy, and myself, that we were safe. But the staff's concern and their warning left me very unsettled. "Lord, I need your help here. I'm not exactly sure what we're up against, but I'm beginning to get the feeling that it's too big for me alone. Please help us. Keep my family from further harm."

For a while we stepped up our vigilance—double-checking the locks at night, watching for strangers in our rearview mirror, and keeping the boys in the backyard to play. We could only speculate as to who and why anyone would want Sandy's videos.

• • •

SCOTT

Life went on in spite of the turmoil. I had resumed my education towards my master's degree in counseling and was finally nearing graduation. Due to the various crises, I had dropped out of the program on at least four occasions. Sandy was still unable to handle much stress. Parenting the boys alone and dealing with random supernatural and human harassments while I was gone often proved too much for her. Many were the times that I would just get settled into class and would suddenly receive a 911 alarm on my pager. After excusing myself from class, I would anxiously hurry to the lobby phone, fearful of what new disaster awaited on the other end of the line. Upon hearing Sandy's frantic report, I would gather my books and rush off for the thirty-minute drive home to deal with the latest emergency.

On one such occasion, I arrived home just in time to find the police at my door. Our son had allegedly defended one of his brothers by attacking a neighbor boy who was picking on him. The other boy's parents had called the police. It must not have been the officer's best night. He came off a little forceful as he explained our son's alleged actions. Sandy, taken off guard by this officer's harsh accusations, reacted by quickly going into a fierce protect mode. After all that had happened to her children, she was not going to stand by and let them be harmed again. I quickly found myself in the middle of a shouting match.

The officer, completely unaware of our family's situation, escalated the confrontation to the point I feared he might forcibly take my wife into custody. That was the last thing I needed.

Standing in the doorway between the protective mama bear and the agitated defender of justice, I knew I had but moments to act. Holding up my hand to keep Sandy at arm's length, I demanded that she go into the other room. I do not know if it was the force of my voice or the steely resolve in my eyes that reached her, but in the end she did as I requested. With Sandy out of the immediate picture, I was finally able to de-escalate the encounter with the officer. Apologizing profusely for my wife, I assured him I would take care of the situation with the neighbor boy. Had I not gotten home when I did, I'm afraid that my normally sweet, demure, law-abiding wife would have been arrested.

After putting out this fire, I walked around the corner to the concerned parents' house and rang the doorbell. The father met me at the door, and I apologized once again, only this time for my son's behavior. Due to the anger my son was dealing with, I knew his actions were more than likely excessive. My apology seemed to be all this worried dad needed to hear. He even suggested that his son most likely played a role in this altercation as well. Things were going well; we struck up a good conversation, in spite of this confrontation being our first introduction to each other. As we talked, we were soon interrupted by this man's older son, who had been riding by on his bicycle. Rushing up to the house, he yelled, "Hey, Dad, there's some chick hiding in the neighbor's bushes, watching you guys!"

Mortified, I had a good idea just who that "chick" was. Quickly excusing myself, I rushed over and gathered my wife from her hiding place in the sparse desert foliage. Holding tightly to her hand, I hurried her home before she could embarrass us further.

On the short walk home Sandy peppered me with a barrage of questions: "Are you okay? Did the neighbor try to get violent? What did he say? What is going to happen now?" It was clear to me this incident had sent her into a tailspin. My irritation with her softened as I realized she believed she was there to protect me. Although still embarrassed, I was thankful that my wife had my back. In our own quirky way, we made a great team.

• • •

SCOTT

It was early 1994. Sandy had regained much of her emotional health. Though her past was not resolved, she had cleared enough painful memories to reorient herself and find some stability. Things had finally calmed to the point that I was able take a position at a Christian counseling center in Phoenix.

Letting go of my painting business in exchange for the work of a counselor was an easy transition. I happily traded in my hot, dirty work truck for a nicely furnished, air-conditioned office. It felt great to be helping people again.

One morning, after only a few months at my new job, I looked out the window to discover a disemboweled rabbit splayed out on the retaining wall right outside my office. *What the heck is going on?* Realizing I had a client coming in soon, I rushed outside to the back of the complex and quickly removed the eviscerated carcass before she arrived.

As I carried the remains to the dumpster, I couldn't help but think there was a connection between this incident and all the other mysterious happenings. Only days before my car had been tampered with while I was working late into the evening, facilitating a men's group. Fortunately, some of the guys stayed after to talk. One of them happened to be a mechanic and was able to repair the damage, allowing me to drive home safely. We had also begun receiving hang-up calls at home. Although they were not life threatening, I wondered if these annoying and upsetting disruptions would ever end. Though we had our suspicions, we did not know for certain who was behind them.

SCOTT

Rousing from a sound sleep one night, I lifted my head off the pillow and attempted to identify the strange noise that had just awakened me. Had it been a part of my dream or was it real? Straining my ear to pick up any unfamiliar sounds, I sat all the way up in bed. My movements woke Sandy, who stared at me through equally sleepy eyes. Noticing my deep concentration, she leaned closer and whispered, "What's wrong?"

"I'm not sure," I absently responded. I was still trying to connect with the illusive noise. "I thought I heard something… something strange."

Sandy joined my vigil. We had grown used to waking to strange sounds at night. Together we sat in the mysterious silence, waiting for the unknown.

"There it is! Is that what you heard?" she exclaimed, the alarm in her voice bleeding through her hushed tone as she anxiously poked me to be certain I had heard it as well.

"Yeah, I'm sure that was it," I whispered. "It sounds like it is coming from outside."

Our bedroom window, which overlooked the backyard, had been cracked open to invite in the cool spring breeze. Only, now it was ushering in these unwanted, eerie rustling sounds.

Quietly sliding out of bed, we crept toward the window. Cautiously opening the glass further, we heard it again. Sure enough, the peculiar noises were coming from the backyard.

"What is it? It sounds really creepy!"

"I don't know. I can't quite make it out. It's like a muffled scream or squawk. Maybe it's even a cat," I said, thumbing through my mental inventory of things that go bump in the night. "I think I hear flapping wings as if something is trying to fly. Could it be a bat? Do bats make noises? Sounds kind of like a bird," I continued, giving voice to my stream of thoughts.

Sandy's tone raised an octave when she suggested, "What if it's a person?"

"I don't know about that," I said. In spite of Sandy's concern, I felt fairly confident these sounds were not emanating from a person.

"Honey, I'm going to call the police!" Sandy panicked as she reached for the wireless phone.

"Wait a minute; let me check it out first."

"Are you sure it's safe? Be careful!" she cautioned as I started out the bedroom door. "Wait, I'm coming with you, and I'll bring the phone, just in case," she said, changing her mind as she rushed to catch up with me in the hall. For good measure, we poked our heads into the boys' room. Thankfully, they were okay this time.

Having grabbed the flashlight and baseball bat that I kept by the bed after recent events, I quietly ventured out into the backyard with Sandy close at my heels. With the faint illumination of a nearby streetlamp, I was able to make out a thrashing mass in the middle of the yard. Readying my flashlight in one hand, my bat in my other, I warily approached this otherworldly bundle. Startled, I jumped back as it writhed and wriggled, the mass convulsing like a maniacal caterpillar attempting to escape its confining bonds. Finally capturing it in the beam of my flashlight, I was shocked to find five terrified roosters bound helplessly together at their legs, each frantically trying to escape the imprisoning tethers. The sounds of their struggles were accompanied by the most pathetic attempts at a cock a doodle doo I had ever heard.

"Oh, my goodness!" came a cry from behind me. I stifled a shudder, startled by Sandy's reaction. I forgot she was so close.

"Don't do that!" I scolded, my jumpiness making my words edgier than I intended.

"I'm sorry," Sandy apologized. "I guess I'm a little spooked. How did they get here all tied up like that?"

"I have no idea." I responded, my adrenal rush beginning to diminish. "They certainly didn't fly here," I retorted, trying to piece together some sort of reasonable explanation for the peculiar scene.

Visions of a strange, evil ritual invaded my mind as I thought of our friend Stan. Stan was a police officer who worked with a special unit that dealt with ritualistic crimes. He had recently shared his concern for us when I told him of some of our strange encounters. These images, and Sandy's question as to how the roosters got here, suddenly had me questioning my certainty that a person was not in our yard. I slowly backed away, instructing Sandy to quickly get into the house. Once inside, with the door securely locked, we worked together to formulate a reasonable explanation. Debating Sandy's earlier suggestion to phone the police, I tried to decide what I would say to them, when my thoughts were interrupted.

"Maybe Uncle Russ left them," Sandy offered.

"That could be," I responded. "But why would he leave them bound like this and in the middle of the night, of all things?" I countered, paranoia still teasing the back of my mind.

"He was probably here late and didn't want to wake us, so he just threw them over the fence all tied together." Sandy's explanation did sound reasonable, reasonable for Uncle Russ that is.

Russ, Sandy's uncle, was kind enough to help us out using his own often unconventional ways. He knew of our financial needs and my own sometimes unusual means of putting food on our table. We had regaled him with tales of my battles with the colossal snapping turtles I caught from the college duck pond. While in school, we were anything but the typical starving students. We feasted from our garden that Sandy planted in a nearby farmer's field. We also dined (Sandy might say gagged) upon the spoils of my crusades against the predatory turtles. Their voracious appetites and aggressive nature marred the otherwise tranquil college landscape. Many a student reported horror stories of lazy afternoons at the pond turning into a scene right out of a *Jaws* movie. The ducks and geese peacefully paddling across the serene waters would suddenly disappear in a violent splash. Students often witnessed the fierce struggle for life taking place just below the surface. It was not uncommon to see orphaned ducklings or one-legged geese and ducks hobbling along the shore.

Incensed by such displays of brutality, the staff and students alike wholeheartedly supported my endeavors. They crowned me with the title "Snapper" for my valiant attempts to save the peaceful, defenseless water fowl from untimely deaths and amputated legs.

Our more recent fiscal problems again spurred my creativity, and I discovered an untapped resource of provisions. The local feed barns often took in undesirable roosters from disappointed people who purchased them as chicks hoping for hens. The aforementioned stock shops often had a surplus of these unwanted roosters and were willing to give them away. Needless to say, I had become fairly adept at preparing these providential offerings for our table.

Please understand that I am an animal lover at heart, so this certainly was not something I enjoyed. Unfortunately, these unwanted fowl were headed for a short existence anyway. I was merely seizing the opportunity to provide what was often the only source of real protein for our growing sons. My early years as a meat department apprentice prepared me for this most undesirable task.

Seeing the rationale of Sandy's theory, I decided to go with the "Uncle Russ" explanation over a possible ritualistic conspiracy scheme. I chose to wait until morning to get confirmation. With that settled, I focused my attention on finding a way to temporarily house the roosters until I returned home that afternoon.

We were relieved when Sandy called her uncle later that morning and confirmed that our pre-dawn guests were indeed a gift from him. He had stopped by earlier in the evening, but we were out running errands. So he secured them in this way to prevent them from flying around the neighborhood.

• • •

SANDY

Scott and I sat anxiously in Kathy's office. She had excused herself shortly after we were seated for my counseling session. When Kathy finally reentered the room, she was accompanied by Mr. Cunningham, the director of the center. Both were wearing grim expressions. I wasn't sure what to make of this new development, but based on the past few years, I assumed this clandestine meeting couldn't be good.

"Scott, Sandy," Kathy began, "Mr. Cunningham is joining us today to fill you in on some recent events that concern you. I'll let him take it from here."

"Good to see you both again," Mr. Cunningham said warmly, shaking our hands. "I just wish it was under better circumstances. We know you both have been through quite an ordeal lately, and we have been quite concerned for you, keeping your family in our prayers. It seems, however, we have come up against a difficult state of affairs ourselves." He paused as if searching for the right words. "There is a lawsuit being filed against our center, and Cat is a part of it. Claims are being made that we are planting false memories in our clients and breaking up families."

I let out an audible gasp at his alarming words. "Cat is suing you?" I couldn't comprehend such a thing. "What an absurd claim to make! No one has planted ideas in my head! I'm so sorry. We had no idea Cat was doing anything like this."

"Don't worry; we know you had nothing to do with this. God will watch over us, and everything will be okay," he tried to assure me. "Our lawyer might need to speak with you, though, if you are up to a meeting."

I said that I would be willing to meet and even offered to write a letter on the center's behalf if that would help. Mr. Cunningham thanked me and assured me that whatever I could do would be very much appreciated.

With that, he left us to begin my counseling session. We continued, in spite of the sense of uncertainty that hung in the air.

The atmosphere at the center over the next few weeks was tense at best, as the counselors were forced to defend their practices and procedures, even that of praying with their clients. The weekly support groups were canceled, and my private sessions with Kathy were strained. Thankfully, we had previously discontinued therapy for our sons; they had progressed as far as they could at their young age, so they were unaffected by these changes.

The letter I wrote in support of the clinic was greatly appreciated, although I'm not certain what impact it had on the case. I eventually worked up the courage to attend one of the hearings, even offering to testify if need be. Scott and I sat together in the relative safety of the back row of the courtroom, all the while praying my testimony would not be necessary.

With a sigh of relief on my part, court adjourned without my testimony.

In the end, Sonrise lost their legal battle and we lost our therapist. Once again, our much-needed support was gone. Though the center offered to provide another counselor, the thought of starting over again with a new therapist was just too disheartening.

• • •

## APRIL 1994

SANDY

Due to the close proximity between our house and Cat's, I wanted to move and put as much distance between us as possible. However, it wasn't until three years after we realized what all Cat had done that it became feasible for us to move. Our house sold after only two months on the market, but we asked the Realtor to forgo the customary "Sold" sign. We wanted to keep the timing of the sale confidential, even though we could not hide the fact that we were, indeed, selling. We were also extremely secretive of the destination of our move, telling only one confidant—our neighbor, my closest friend.

One day as I was packing, the doorbell rang. I startled at the sound, wondering who was on the other side of the door. Chiding myself for my jumpiness, I decided it was most likely my neighbor who had been helping me pack. She probably forgot something and was returning to retrieve it. Convinced that was the case, I opened the door to my friend.

The woman who stood before me was not at all who I expected. *Oh great, I should have checked the peephole. Now I have to deal with a solicitor.* The thought had barely completed before the woman started in.

"Hello, I am Celeste, the executive producer for (a nationally known evening world-news reporter)," the animated business woman proclaimed, thrusting her business card into my hesitant hand.

I was surprised and confused as to why this executive producer was standing on my doorstep. Wouldn't a phone call have been sufficient? Bob had called several times. Though I did not like receiving the calls, at least they were not as disconcerting as having someone here in person. I was further bewildered that a producer for such a well-known broadcast-news celebrity would be interested in me. I was so narrowly focused that I still could not believe my breakdown could cause such a stir. I could not understand or grasp Cat's intentions in making our problems such a public matter.

Celeste must have read the confusion on my face as she continued. "We are developing a unique news program that will be hosted by (her client and a second reporter with equal national recognition). Your story has come across my desk, and I must say, we were quite intrigued. We would like to feature you in our upcoming programming."

*Here we go again,* I thought, as I blanked out the rest of her sales pitch. I was weary of all the prompting to "tell my side of the story." I just wanted everyone to go away. I mustered my confidence and said, "I'm going to have to decline. I really do not want to be featured on any television program, no matter who is doing the interviewing. Thank you for coming; have a good day." I moved to shut the door when she quickly added, "I can see that you are moving soon. I'd like to get your new address so I can contact you once you are settled."

There was no way was I going to give away our carefully guarded secret. Our move was finally an opportunity to leave this turmoil behind and begin a new life. Why in the world would I invite these people to follow us? I respectfully explained that we were not giving out that information and politely shut the door. I could hear her continued urging as I set the lock and headed back to my packing.

I smiled as I filled each box with what was left of our worldly possessions after having sold so much to pay the mounting bills. Yet, not even the frustration with the uninvited solicitor could dampen my hopes. I was overflowing with anticipation for the freedom, protection, and anonymity our new life would afford.

# SURVIVAL SKILL

## #2

# *Look for the Good*

> Every detail in our lives of love for God is worked into something good.
>
> Romans 8:28 MSG

SCOTT

"The world has yet to see what God can do through one man who is totally devoted to him. God willing, I will be that man!" The passion and commitment in this declaration stirred something deep within me. *That is the desire of my heart,* I thought as I hungrily devoured the words on the page before me from the biography *The Life and Work of D.L. Moody* by J. W. Chapman. [1] I was a college freshman at the time and eager to make my mark upon the world. I admired the way Moody impacted the lives of many through his somewhat unconventional methods. Though we were separated by more than a century, I was drawn to this man who was completely devoted to the Lord. I determined, like him, to be a world changer. *God, I completely commit my life to you as this great man did. Work in me to help others as you worked in Moody.*

SANDY

Like Scott, I too had a spiritually defining moment, only mine came as a precocious three-year-old. Although it was at such a tender age, the indelible memory of this significant moment is forever etched in both my heart and mind. Seldom left in the nursery, I sat with my parents through most church services. As this particular meeting came to a close, our pastor invited those who needed prayer to come forward. God was wooing my little heart that day. Soon I was offering that heart to Jesus while my pastor listened to my prayer. In that moment, I felt a calling and a sense that God had a unique plan for my life.

In the years since my breakdown, I've often wondered if the reason I gave my heart to Jesus as such a small child was because of the abuse I was enduring at that time. It gives me comfort to believe that I experienced the presence of Jesus in those dark hours.

Scott and I met the summer of 1980, not two weeks after my high-school graduation. Drawn by our shared passion to be used by God, we embarked on a journey of service and were married the following summer.

This life of helping others, though rewarding, has not always been easy. After five years of ministry, three births, and one miscarriage, the strain of life took a toll on my health. At the time, I had no idea that these stressors were merely the tip of the iceberg. The real problems lay deeply buried under the darkened sea of blotted memories.

Our initial enthusiasm tarnished as the stresses of the ministry mounted. Then we were both pushed to the breaking point when, during the process of merging our church with another body of believers, several insurmountable problems occurred.

Suddenly the highly anticipated union crumbled before it even began. Exhausted and disillusioned, we decided it was time for a much-needed recuperative rest. In spite of the many pleas that we stay, we felt it best that we resign.

SCOTT

This decision, though necessary, left us jobless. Consequently, in October of 1988, we packed up our young family (the boys ranging in age from two to five) and headed to Arizona where employment as the foreman of a painting crew awaited me. The plan was to take a one-year sabbatical and return to the ministry. As our year of rest came to an end, Sandy was much improved but still a long way from her typical strong, vibrant self. We sent out résumés anyway; much to our dismay, we received no offers.

The first year soon melded into the second. Our one-year sabbatical began to feel more like a life sentence. It was as though God was finished with us and had cast us aside, into the desert—literally. We sacrificed so much to do all that we believed God had asked of us. Now, three years later, we were to suffer more loss and disappointment. It seemed that the God we loved so deeply and to whom we had dedicated our very lives had abandoned us. How much was one family supposed to take?

My disillusionment with the ministry now carried over into my personal relationship with God. An inner conflict began to rage. Part of me still trusted God regardless of the setbacks and chaos; but another part doubted and questioned him to the point of anger. I seriously wondered if he cared about us any longer. My mind chastised me for my distrust, arguing that God was still in control. My heart, though, felt differently. I couldn't help feeling disappointed and let down. My dreams and sense of purpose were crushed. The safety, protection, and blessing that my family had previously experienced were suddenly gone, ripped from their very foundations.

SANDY

The struggles intensified, coming at a rapid-fire rate; we had no opportunity to bounce back from one problem before another exploded. Under such pressure, we began to wonder what we had done to warrant such problems. In those rare moments when we could actually catch our breath, we often dove into deep introspection, searching our past and the Scriptures for answers. We always strived to live the kind of lives that would be pleasing to God. Although we certainly had flaws and had made more than our fair share of mistakes, we could not understand what we had done to bring such trauma and pain into our lives.

## When Bad Becomes Good

SCOTT AND SANDY

Though we felt like giving up, we didn't. We pushed through. It took time, prayer, and study, but eventually our trust, faith in God, and hope for our family's future were restored. At the time we prayed for a miracle, hoping for an instant fix. However, change did not come that quickly. Instead, through our journey, we rediscovered a foundational key that helped pull us out of our despair. Although it was a concept that we had known and practiced for years, we had lost sight of this truth due to the weightiness of our experiences and the accelerated pace at which they occurred.

As we began to catch our breath, God reminded us of an important principle that became our second Survival Skill: *Looking for the Good.*

The concept of *good* is based in Romans 8:28, which states, "And we know that in all things God works for the good of those who love him, who have been called according to His purpose" (NIV). The Message Bible puts it this way: "We can be sure that every detail in our lives of love for God is worked into something good." According to this scripture, for those of us who are believers, God takes our mistakes, limitations, and weaknesses, as well as the bad and painful things that happen to us, and works them into something *good.* For those who haven't yet come to this place, God may be using painful experiences to draw you to him. God lets nothing go to waste; even our darkest hours and deepest pains are used to create good in our lives.

Even those troubles that are forced upon us with the cruelest of intentions are not beyond God's reach. As we worked through our painful emotions, the only real hope we found came again from Scripture. Joseph's story in the book of Genesis gained realism for us, as we found ourselves relating to his suffering. We were encouraged by the way God turned his painful experiences and injustices with direct intent to harm into something good. And it was not just for Joseph's good, but it extended to his family and an entire nation.

As you may remember, Joseph, the youngest son of a large family, was clearly his father's favorite. This favoritism sparked serious jealousy and resentment among his older brothers. Joseph only exacerbated this resentment when he shared a dream of his family bowing at his feet. His brothers responded by plotting to kill him. But God intervened. His brothers ultimately sold him into slavery and deceived their father into believing he was dead.

Because of his brothers' evil intentions, Joseph spent many years as a slave and prisoner. Joseph's wisdom and God-given gift of interpreting dreams eventually earned him a place in Pharaoh's court. From his new position, he instituted a policy of "saving for a rainy day." The kingdom began storing away grain in preparation for an impending drought. When the drought finally came, the policy paid off, saving the lives of thousands. His brothers were among those citizens looking for the life-saving provisions. Not recognizing Joseph, they bowed before him, thus fulfilling God's prophecy. Rather than turn them away in anger and vengeance, Joseph gave them what they needed. Later, when they recognized him, they feared for their lives, but Joseph alleviated their fears by stating, "You planned evil against me but God used those same plans for my good" (Genesis 50:2 MSG). The plans themselves were not *good,* but God brought about *good* from them.

We can share in the hope and knowledge that even in our most desperate moments, our pain is never in vain. We do not suffer merely for the sake of suffering. God leverages our hardships for our benefit. Even though we might not always see or understand what the good is in our lifetime, we can know that God is faithful to keep his promise and will create good from our pain.

God is faithful to bring about something
good from our pain.

---

# IT'S YOUR TURN

SCOTT AND SANDY

What about you? Are you struggling to see how God could bring about any good from your difficult circumstances? Perhaps you too find yourself dealing with a life that has been thrown into chaos. Maybe your faith is wavering. You want to trust God, but you're struggling. Perhaps you are even angry with him. You might even feel guilty for having these doubts and frustrations. Don't lose hope; read on.

## A Vision Issue

Did you know that your inability to see God working the good into your life is actually a vision issue? God's good is present in your life whether you recognize it or not. Good does not magically appear just because you notice it, nor does good cease to be present when you do not see it. Not looking for the good merely robs you of the benefits of experiencing the good. This further prevents you from finding any meaning in your suffering. When you align your sight with God, you can trust that everything he allows into your life will be there for a purpose—a good purpose.

Common visual problems that keep us from seeing the good in our life.

Check off any that apply.

- ☐ I focus more on what is wrong with my life than on what is right.
- ☐ I view God as a condemning, punishing dictator who is just waiting to punish me whenever I step out of line.
- ☐ I tend to see things in terms of black and white, right or wrong, and good or bad.
- ☐ I equate *good* with ease, pleasure, and blessing. I equate *bad* with pain, struggle, and punishment.
- ☐ I view life through a cynical lens.
- ☐ I believe that I've messed things up so badly that there is no way God can possibly bring any good out of my life.
- ☐ I struggle to be thankful.
- ☐ I tend to see the glass half-empty.
- ☐ I entertain worst-case scenarios.
- ☐ I tend to catastrophize, awfulize, and overdramatize.

## Corrective Measures

Just as there are corrective lenses, exercises, and even surgeries that can improve your physical vision, there are also corrective measures you can take to improve and adjust your insight or "trust" vision.

## *Look for the Good*

The first step in improving your ability to see the good in your trials is to determine to actively look for the good. Looking for the good in your life is a choice. You can choose to find the good that is present, or you can choose not to. Just remember that regardless of what you decide, God's good does not cease to exist because you choose not to see. Nor does it suddenly become good the moment you see it as such. God's good always exists, whether you choose to acknowledge it or not.

Though you will not always be able to identify the specific good that is present, choosing to trust God and believing he will bring about good from your difficult experiences are what is truly important. This is the type of faith, or "trust vision," spoken of in Hebrews 11:1: "Being sure of what we hope for and certain of what we do not see" (NIV).

God's good exists in our lives whether
or not we choose to see it.

## *Normalize Your Struggles*

We all have our ups and downs; they are a natural part of life. Stuff happens! Whatever our status in Christ, none are exempt from problems and difficult experiences. We discovered this firsthand. There were many times we felt we were being singled out. However, we came to realize that having problems in life was normal.

Peter confirms this in 1 Peter 4:12, where he encourages us by saying "Don't be surprised at the painful trials you are suffering as though something strange were happening to you" (NIV). From this passage we find that not only are struggles natural, but they are to be expected. The good news is that God has promised not to allow anything to happen beyond your ability to endure, even though you may feel otherwise. He knows how far you can go in your own strength and how far you can stretch while relying on him (1 Corinthians 10:13). His desire is that you partner with him and not simply rely on your own abilities.

## *Shift Your Focus from What's Wrong to What's Right*

There is something in our human nature that has a tendency to focus on the negative and overlook the positives in life, especially when we feel held captive by our circumstances. The problem is: what we focus on is often what we get.

If you hold a spotlight on everything that is wrong in your life, that is all you will see. Those things that are good and right will be forced into the shadows and selectively overlooked. This discriminatory way of looking at life will only serve to keep you stuck in a negative, depressed, or pessimistic outlook. Hope will continue to elude you. However, with a renewed perspective, you can now actively seek out what is right. Look for it; it is there!

When you focus on the negative, that is all you will see.

## *Stop Catastophizing and Awfulizing*

When we are suffering, we can easily overdramatize our circumstances, making them feel and appear worse than they really are. Problems are often difficult enough without us making them more disastrous.

When you find yourself awfulizing your circumstances, stop and tell yourself, "Though I feel that things may not be good, they are probably not as bad as I'm making them out to be." Even if your circumstances are actually as bad as they appear, you can draw strength from God's many promises to bring about good through these trials (Romans 5:3–5).

## *Find Meaning in Your Suffering*

People often ask us how we overcame so many seemingly insurmountable obstacles. The answer is simple but was not always easy. We looked for the meaning in—not necessarily the answers to—our distress. Does that mean we didn't search for answers? No. As we've previously shared, we confronted our whys, both the curious and the non-accepting variety. In the end, however, we discovered that the opportunity for change is found in the search for meaning more than in the search for answers.

Finding meaning in our suffering provided us with a sense of purpose behind that suffering. This purpose motivated us to make our experiences count for something more. We leveraged our trials and therefore, maximized them for our own personal growth and maturity. This made it possible for us to more effectively navigate through our future difficulties and to help others with theirs.

We encourage you to find meaning and purpose in your own suffering. Consider how you might make your painful experiences count for something more. If you are having difficulty finding meaning in your suffering, ask God to help you discover it.

Your obstacles are opportunities in disguise.

## *View Your Obstacles as Opportunities*

Did you know that obstacles are actually opportunities in disguise? James 1:2–4 puts it this way: "Consider it a sheer gift, friends, when tests and challenges (*obstacles*) come at you from all sides. You know that under pressure, your faith-life is forced into the open and shows its true colors. So don't try to get out of anything prematurely. Let it do its work (*opportunity*) so you become mature and well-developed, not deficient in any way" (MSG, emphasis ours).

What differentiates obstacles from opportunities is your perspective. How you view your challenge will determine whether you respond or react to it. If you view it as an obstacle, your reaction will be to fight against it. However, when you see your struggle as an opportunity, you can respond to it and maximize the benefits of God's intended purposes behind it.

Consider these questions:

- What opportunities are presenting themselves to you though your circumstances?
- In what ways may they be intended to improve your life?
- How might God be using them to mature and complete you?
- What are some ways you might benefit from your circumstances to help accomplish these goals?

## *Adopt an Attitude of Gratitude*

Gratitude is one of the surest ways to help you focus on the *good* in your life, especially during those times when *good* is difficult to see. Gratitude simply means being thankful and appreciative. In 1 Thessalonians 5:18 we are advised to be thankful in all of our circumstances—both positive and negative. We are not told to simply have a feeling of thankfulness, but rather to develop an attitude of gratefulness in and through our pain. This attitude is developed through a determination to be grateful.

What can you be grateful for, even in the midst of your troubling circumstances? Are you ready to be stretched? Try this on: Take those things for which you are resentful and ask God to help you find something to be grateful for in them. This may feel like too much of a stretch, but you can bend this far by believing that God is doing something good in and through your pain.

Perhaps you have suffered a tremendous loss and the thought of finding gratitude *in* (not necessarily *for*) that loss may feel well beyond your capacity at this point. You might even be angry. That is natural. There is a grieving process we each must go through with the losses we experience. The greater the loss, the more time it takes. If you are not yet able to take this step, that is okay. Be easy on yourself. Give yourself time. You will know when you are ready to take that next step. Remember, God loves you and he understands your pain. Even though you may not feel it at this point, just believe that somehow, some way, he will bring good from your heartache.

## *Finding Good*

We admit that our own journey has been a bumpy one. Sometimes it has been difficult to see the good in our struggles. We have not always done it well. Sometimes we have not done it at all.

Even though God was working our experience for our good, we could have missed seeing it. Because we believed him and chose to focus on *his* working, not Cat's, we were able to experience healing and growth. Had we remained fixated on Cat and the troubles we were having, we might well have remained stuck and embittered.

What we've shared of our story thus far might have you wondering what good could come from it. You might be surprised to see how God can take the misguided and even evil intentions of others, as well as any difficult or traumatic circumstance, and work them out for good.

Let us share some of our own with you:

- Admittedly, we were devastated when our church merger fell apart. At the time it felt as though we were taking giant steps backward rather than traveling forward in our journey. However, we came to realize that God used this experience to prepare us for his redirection and for what was to come. We believed we were meant to help people through a church ministry, but his plan was to use us to help others in different capacities.

- When we were told that the recordings of Sandy's personal counseling sessions were stolen from the counseling center, we felt violated and exposed. As time went by, however, hindsight enabled us to see the good. At the time we agreed to allow Sandy to be recorded, we were in a survival mode. Sonrise's offer to provide free counseling in exchange for those recorded sessions was too good to pass up. The upside of the theft is that these tapes are not being publicly shown in training workshops, which was their intended purpose. This sort of display would be extremely embarrassing and completely incongruent with Sandy's life today. Even though we do not know the whereabouts of these stolen recordings, we trust that God has this situation under his control. This might be one of those situations where we will not actually see the good this side of heaven. In spite of the unknown, we choose to believe that this too is good.
- When Sonrise Counseling Center lost their legal battle and informed us that Sandy could no longer see Kathy for counseling, Sandy was devastated. How could losing our trusted counselor who helped us navigate through our difficulties be good? There had to be an upside, and there was. Sandy had been in intensive therapy for three years; it was time for a break. What she needed most at that point was to try her hand at simply living and enjoying life. This proved to be the next stage in her recovery and was equally as helpful as the first.
- Being asked by Pastor Lou to leave our church home was equally devastating for us. Not only did we feel abandoned by the very people we considered our church

family, but it felt as though we were once again being thrown to the curb. We harbor no ill feelings toward Pastor Lou or his church. Though we were deeply hurt, we understand that pastors are human too. Personally, as a young, inexperienced, idealistic pastor, I made my own fair share of mistakes. The reality was, our needs were extreme and his small church was not equipped to deal with them. If it were not for the pastor's conversation with Scott, we might not have left this church. As a result, we would have missed out on the specialized support we received through Pastor Douglas and his congregation. Although we didn't see it at the time, this change was also for our good.

- The strange and bizarre incidents that manifested in our home really threw us for a loop. Both of us came from backgrounds that provided us with little, if any, understanding or experience in dealing with these hellish encounters. As a result of this battle, Scott realized how his previous vow to no longer count on God's protection but to defend our family himself was woefully inadequate. This realization was pivotal in his returning the responsibility for our protection and safety back to God. With our new friends' and church's help, we learned how to competently handle these otherworldly experiences. These spiritual struggles gave us a deeper understanding of this realm and equipped us with the tools necessary to handle it.
- Some of the out-of-the-ordinary events in our lives provided us with a balanced view between what was actually a spiritual attack and what were simply strangely peculiar experiences.
- Sandy's embarrassing incident with the police officer and subsequent hiding in the neighbor's bushes provided her an opportunity to work through her embar-

rassment and shame. She eventually realized that, at that time, she was acting from a very wounded and protective place. In her panicked and confused state, she was trying to protect our family. Since then, she has experienced much healing and growth. Naturally, she would now respond to that situation in a much different manner. Having previously held herself to a rigid standard that did not allow for mistakes, she is now able to let go of the shame associated with her past actions and can embrace the funny side of her own life lessons. We both have since enjoyed several good laughs at her uncharacteristic antics on that eventful evening.

- Finding any good from the trauma brought about by the variety of abuses we experienced was, without a doubt, the most difficult challenge of all. We did not know if we could ever see any good coming from the devastating breach of trust and the evil that was inflicted upon us. We naturally struggled with anger, rage, disappointment, hurt, astonishment, and yes, even forgiveness. Our biggest breakthrough occurred when we connected with Joseph's story in Genesis 50. Feeling a kindred spirit with Joseph and his suffering, we couldn't help but believe that God would take the harm that was imposed upon us and transform it for our good and the good of others, just as he did for Joseph. And God did just that. He has used these experiences to develop within us a deeper level of insight, understanding, compassion, and a nonjudgmental attitude toward others who are suffering.

## CONCLUSION

It is important to realize that the specific *good* is not always immediately visible. For Joseph, it was fourteen years before he realized the purpose behind his suffering. For us, the timing of our seeing the good has varied. In some areas we saw it more rapidly than in others. Situations remain where we have not yet seen the good and might never in our lifetime. Keep in perspective that actually being able to determine the specific good is not of utmost importance. Trusting that God is working, and therefore, living your life within that understanding, is the imperative.

Remember, like Joseph, you don't have to let the tough times beat you. As a believer, you can know beyond a shadow of a doubt that whatever it is you are experiencing or have experienced, God will work it all into something *good.*

# *No Escape*

SANDY

The move was exhausting but worth every strained muscle and sore back. We were finally free! Scott continued working six days a week at the counseling center and was enjoying every minute. His commute went from over fifty minutes to less than fifteen. Though our new home was a step down from our former house, we were grateful for a fresh start. In spite of its smaller 1,100 square feet, the house sported four bedrooms, giving each of the boys a room of their own. They spent hours arranging their personal space and exploring their new neighborhood. My chronic fatigue continued to flare, but in spite of the limited energy reserves, my outlook was bright and hopeful. Our lives were beginning anew!

We had been in our new home almost two weeks when my seemingly endless task of unpacking was interrupted by a ring of the doorbell. I was pleasantly surprised at my reaction—the normal worry knot did not automatically form in my stomach.

I was actually excited to see who was at my door. Anticipation welled at the possibility of a welcome from a new neighbor. Quickly brushing my hands through my hair, I hoped I looked somewhat presentable. I pushed several empty boxes out of the way so this new friend and I might have room to sit and chat for a moment. Grabbing hold of the knob, I smiled as I pulled the door open. The look of shock that consumed my face was anything but a greeting for the person on my doorstep. This was no friendly neighbor awaiting me.

Jennie, a friend I'd met through the group at the counseling center, was at my door. A friend, that is, until she and her family participated in the lawsuit against the center and forged a bond with Cat, knowing full well the abuse and torment this person had inflicted on my family and me.

Jennie spoke before I could find my own voice. "Hi, Sandy." Her cheerful greeting disguised the strained relationship we now shared. I stepped outside to join her, shutting the door behind me. My past might have found me, but it would not be welcome in my new home.

"Hi, Jennie, um ... I don't mean to be rude, but how did you find us?" I asked, completely astounded that she had discovered our new location, and so quickly, at that.

"Oh, that was easy; your former neighbor was more than happy to tell me," she gloated.

The knife of betrayal twisted in my heart once again. I began to feel as though I was a major failure in choosing friends, especially those in whom I confided. It troubled me that my friend and neighbor had given away our new location, but I wasn't completely surprised. The day of our move something had changed between us, something I did not understand. Nonetheless, I hadn't expected that she would share this important information.

Jennie chatted on about her recent move out of state and how much fun she and her children were having while vacationing at Cat's house. It was clear she was subtly trying to entice me as she regaled the narrative of their many adventures. Indeed, there was often much enjoyment to be had at Cat's house, and Jennie knew how devoid of such pleasure our lives had become. Eventually she got to the point and finished the message she had been sent to deliver: "Cat wants you to know that *when* you leave Scott, you will be welcomed back with open arms."

I nearly snorted, stifling a laugh at such a ridiculous invitation. Her definitive use of the word *when,* not *if,* didn't escape me either. "Are you serious? Why would I leave the husband I love for someone who hurt and abused my family and me? No, thank you!"

The conversation soon ended. As Jennie left, I stepped back into the house. Once inside, I set the lock and leaned against the wall for support. Our safely guarded secret had vanished before my very eyes. A dark cloud of apprehension smothered my hopes and joy of a fresh start. Our location was known, and there was no way to reclaim the privacy we worked so diligently to ensure.

• • •

SANDY

Spring gave way to the hot Arizona summer. There were no more unexpected haunts from our past, yet we found it difficult to let down our guard. Our sons adjusted to their new surroundings, but they missed their old friends and discovered summer to be a difficult time to find new ones. I too missed friends, but we soon found a church and began forging new relationships.

When fall rolled around I was reluctant to entrust my sons to their new school, in spite of its close proximity to our house—our front door looked out onto the playground. Our heightened concern for the boys' safety persisted. We presented the principal and office personnel with a photo of Cat and made it clear that our sons were never to be released to anyone other than ourselves. I became involved in each of their classrooms, helping their teachers as much as possible. The boys enjoyed having me near and often came to the schoolyard fence on their lunch break, calling to me until I stepped out of the house and waved. A highlight during this difficult time was the special bond that developed within our family.

Though many of our strange experiences had finally died down, the lingering effects of our trials remained. Our one son's occasional sleepwalking, though it lessened in frequency, still kept us diligent about his safety at night. Unless stopped, he would get up, dress, and head out the front door as if he had somewhere to go or someone to meet. Another of our sons began to struggle with extreme anxiety; we sought to foster an inner confidence and a sense of safety for him. A battle with obsessive thoughts began to plague our other son.

One day this son came to us saying he needed to run away. He didn't understand why, but he had to leave immediately. Scott and I had always diligently prayed for wisdom in helping our hurting children, and this time was no different. We needed to act quickly. There was no telling what our son might do in this frame of mind, as he had become quite compulsive during this time. The fact that he might disappear was a very real concern. We racked our brains for a quick, creative solution for this child who felt compelled to escape his pain in such a dangerous way. As we prayed, I was struck with an inventive idea. I ran it by Scott, and he agreed that we should give it a shot. Walking into our son's room, we presented him with the plan: "Honey, we have an idea for you. I know you feel you need to run away, but... what if Dad sets up the tent in the backyard, where you can stay all by yourself for as long as you need? You can keep your own supply of food and water in your tent. We will buy you a special notebook where you can write down all your troubling thoughts. It will be like running away, but you will be safe. What do you think?"

He agreed to give it a try, so we set up his little space in the safety of our fenced-in yard. Relieved of his compulsion to escape, his "run away" lasted only a couple of days. Although his eleven-year-old mind and emotions still struggled with the pain and trauma of his abuse, his need to run subsided.

This was but one example of the creative parenting we engaged to help our sons in their recovery processes. My own healing continued, as well. I enjoyed months at a time of relative normality. Yet all it would take was a certain odor, a particular touch, a few days of cloudy weather, selective scenes from television or a movie, or having my startle response engaged, and I would once again succumb to depression and anxiety. These PTSD (post traumatic stress disorder)-induced bouts of melancholy were unwelcome interruptions in my life. There were times I could pull out of this state within a matter of days; at other times it would take a few weeks. Thankfully, the hours I put into my recovery were paying off and I increasingly gained the ability to bounce back.

• • •

SANDY

During the first year of my breakdown, Scott had applied for Social Security Disability benefits on my behalf. Acceptance was immediate, and my supervision under Dr. Morrison was replaced by a revolving door of state-funded psychiatrists and social workers. Though it was often difficult dealing with so many changes, we were grateful for the cost-free care. Our recent move required another such change; however, with three years of therapy and psychiatric visits behind me, the change was a relatively easy one. For the last few years, my visits to the state clinic were decreased to once every six months. I did well under the limited care because I was determined to be well. I continued working on my own recovery: journaling, processing feelings, praying for healing, and restructuring my thought processes. Scott was a tremendous help during this time. He was always willing to talk with me and help me work through my difficulties. This journey was not easy for him. For the first two years of therapy, he sat in on nearly every session and was exposed to all the grizzly details of my memories, details, and images that were impossible to erase.

During this time, Scott was gaining the reputation of a compassionate counselor with a unique ability to disarmingly speak truth to his clients. Though he enjoyed working at the center and the friendships he'd forged with colleagues there, he felt God calling him to start his own counseling business. So, after a year and a half in this new profession, and a year in our new home, we converted our garage into a nice office with an outside entrance and its own bathroom, a perfect home office for Scott. In the comfort of my own home and at the leisure of my own pace, I assumed the role of office manager, answering phones and billing insurance.

Scott was asked to speak one Thursday night at a Celebrate Recovery group in one of Phoenix's larger churches. Together, we presented a humorous skit before Scott dove into the meaty material. Following the meeting, we were greeted by many people. One of the women introduced herself to me as Samantha. She was a local counselor who donated an evening once a week to the recovery group. Sam and I developed an immediate connection. We gathered up a couple of chairs, and I spent the next hour getting to know Sam and her client-empowering approach to counseling. The more she spoke, the more excited I became. Had I finally found the right individual to help me through the next step in my healing process? I decided Scott and I would spend the next few days praying about this.

The professionals at the Sonrise Counseling Center had truly saved my life, and for that I will be eternally grateful. I was now ready for the next phase in my progress, and the more we prayed, the more Sam's approach seemed to be just what I needed.

Within a week's time I was sitting in Samantha's office, eager to begin. Sam's unique style and helpful techniques allowed me to sit in the driver's seat of my own recovery, which was important for me at this stage.

A few months into counseling, the movie *The Matrix* hit the big screen. Being science fiction and action fans, we were eager to see this revolutionary film with its innovative action sequences. Transfixed to the screen, I soon found myself identifying with the character Neo, played by Keanu Reeves. Neo was awakened one day to the truth about his life: it was nothing more than a simulated reality. What he, and all of humanity, believed to be true was nothing but a grand illusion created to keep them quietly pacified—the Matrix. In reality, each person was kept unconscious in individualized pods while the machine-controlled world fueled itself through the energy and heat their placid bodies generated.

Neo's life closely mirrored my own in its confusing and disjointed reality. We both had embarked on an incredible journey to uncover and live in the truth. When Morpheus, the leader of the resistance, said to Neo in his deep, hypnotic voice, "This is your last chance. After this, there is no turning back," I leaned forward in my seat, not wanting to miss a beat. "You take the blue pill, the story ends, you wake up in your bed, and believe whatever you want to believe. You take the red pill, you stay in Wonderland and I show you how deep the rabbit hole goes." I was lost in the scene with Neo and Morpheus. As Neo swallowed, I too was swallowing, nearly choking on, the red pill—the pill of truth; the reality of my past. The movie suddenly became unsettling and difficult to watch. I was tumbling down the rabbit hole, trying to understand my own matrix.

The next week, Samantha and I talked about how I felt the movie mirrored my own life in its eerie significance. Did I want, as Neo did, to continue to push through the discomfort of knowing the reality of my past? Was I willing to fully embrace the truth, or did I want to believe that which was comforting, the illusion that I had a safe and healthy childhood, even if it might be a lie?

This dilemma was nothing new for me; the movie had simply brought it all together in a very unique way. Numerous times on my journey I had come to these very crossroads, and each time, though difficult, I chose to swallow the uncomfortable truth.

What was new, however, was that accepting this truth at this deeper level created a type of identity crisis. Who am I? Am I an abused and broken person, or am I a healthy, whole person?

Samantha challenged me: "Does the core of who you are—the individual God made—change because of your past?" She nudged me further: "Are you any more or less of a person because of what happened?"

The questions stopped me cold. *Am I any more or less of a person because of my past?* After a few thoughtful moments, I answered, "My past has influenced my thoughts and beliefs. Knowing what happened is important. It has helped make sense of several things that troubled me. The bottom line is *who* I am is not based solely on what happened to me. I am the *me* God created, whether I was abused or not."

Samantha went on to explain that the core of who I am was created by God before I was even born (Psalm 139:13–16). She clarified that a person's past can, and does, affect them, but it does not completely alter their basic personality. "And, at the time of your breakdown, you were who you were, regardless of what you knew or remembered. The same goes for the present. Helping you connect with your past only helps you understand why you react to certain stimuli, why your thoughts take you in certain directions, but you remain *who* you are. Your past does not identify you. Your value and significance have absolutely nothing to do with what happened to you."

Our discussion was comforting and went a long way toward helping me settle my identity problem. I did not have to view myself in the strict context of an abuse victim. This revelation was pivotal. I was at a crossroads in my healing. Realizing I could accept my former chaos without identifying myself with it gave me the freedom I needed to continue to move forward. The more I experienced life from this healthier place, the more empowerment and self-affirmation I felt. I was becoming comfortable showing up in the world as me, the Sandy God created, unburdened, not untouched, by my experiences.

• • •

SCOTT

"Honey, I need to talk to you, but you might want to sit down," Sandy said. It always made me nervous when she began a conversation with this preface. "That phone call was from John. Yeah, I know, I was shocked too," she added in response to my look of surprise. "He and Stacie want to meet with us. They said they have some questions and want to hear our side of the story. I'm a bit nervous. It's been so long, but I would really like to see them again. What do you think?"

Wow! I was stunned. Though I had missed John and Stacie, I never thought we would hear from them or the rest of Sandy's family again. The last time we talked was when we called family members, warning them about the danger Cat posed to their children, the danger that we had failed to recognize with our own kids. In that phone call it was made very clear that John and Stacie did not want to talk to us. It was obvious from their response that Cat had gotten to them first. Cat could be very persuasive, and God only knows what was said to them. Sandy had been devastated by this added rejection. I silently reflected on this conversation; it seemed a lifetime had come and gone since it took place.

"Well, what do you think?" Sandy inquired, interrupting my thoughts.

"Hmm . . . I don't know," I replied, a bit skeptical and worried that Sandy would get hurt again. "Why, all of the sudden, do they want to talk to us? They haven't spoken to us in seven years."

"I don't know, honey," Sandy responded. "I just want to give them a chance and hear them out. I know we are taking a risk, but this could be God working to reconcile our relationships. It has been awfully lonely without any family contact. I miss the big family holidays. I hate that we don't know who we can trust. But John sounded so sincere over the phone. I really would like to do this."

"I guess you could be right about God reconciling," I concluded. I knew Sandy valued family and had deeply missed John and Stacie. "It's your family, so it's your call," I conceded, knowing what her decision would be.

Plans were made to meet in a neutral location: a restaurant halfway between us. Arriving at nearly the same moment, our initial reunion was awkward. After seven years, so much had happened; so much had changed. It was obvious that we could not trust Cat. Could we trust John and Stacie, or was this just another way for Cat to disrupt our lives?

In spite of our hesitations, by the time our salads arrived we began warming up to each other and John felt comfortable enough to present their questions.

"Over the last several months we have seen discrepancies in things Cat has told us, and this gives us cause to doubt and question the validity of what we've been told concerning you," John began. "We decided the best way to deal with this was to hear your side of the story."

*It's about time!* I caught myself before the reactive words left my mouth. Though I wanted to reconnect, I was struggling with my feelings.

Successfully resisting my impulsive words, I endeavored to look inquisitive rather than accusatory. Sandy took my hand under the table for support and invited them to "fire away," as we had nothing to hide.

Clearing his throat to rid himself of his obvious discomfort, John began. "Scott, is it true that you broke into Cat's house, stole valuables, and rummaged through drawers in order to find and take letters that Sandy had written?"

I thought I was braced for anything, but right out of the chute I was floored by the absurdity of such a claim. I was shocked at the accusation and even more so at the fact that it had been believed. Before I could respond, however, Sandy interrupted: "What letters?"

"The letters in which you said you wanted to leave Scott because he was abusive to you," Stacie interjected.

Now even more stunned than before, I was relieved when Sandy articulated, in no uncertain terms, that I had never laid a hand on her physically or emotionally. She further disputed the existence of any letters.

Shaking off my shock, I requested details about this supposed break-in and infamous letter heist.

John and Stacie began recounting the story as they heard it. Not long into the tale, they looked at each other incredulously as they listened to the lunacy of their own words. It was as though a spell had been broken. The farther into the story they got, the crazier and oddly staged they found it to be. Not much of a defense was required before we all found ourselves laughing and making jokes about my supposed criminal venture.

With the tension broken, we settled on their sincerity; this was not a ploy intended to harm us. We could see they sincerely wanted the truth, so we encouraged them to continue with their questions. Stacie and John actually seemed relieved to hear the facts truthfully presented and assured us that they believed us. We too were relieved that their eyes had finally been opened and that they were receptive to the truth.

Cleared on all counts of the break-in, they moved to the next accusation they'd been told. "Were you kicked out of your church for embezzling funds?"

The church in question was the one in which I had previously served as senior pastor. The stunned look on my face had to be noticeable. Shocked again to hear such an outlandish lie, it took me a second or two to recover my thoughts. Collecting myself, I explained that I had resigned from the church for a variety of reasons—my own burn-out, the merger falling apart, and Sandy's health issues. I assured them that I was not fired, nor was I kicked out. As a matter of fact, the leadership and most of the congregation, beyond the few who were unhappy with the merger, begged us to stay, but we felt it was time to move on. It was important to get Sandy into a less stressful environment. I went on to share that in order to remain above board in all respects I intentionally kept my name off the church's bank accounts. I never even had access to the church's money.

I was relieved once again to find that they both believed me. It felt good to have the opportunity to refute these lies; nonetheless, I found it disturbing that Cat had spread such slanderous rumors in the first place. What could have prompted such maliciousness? I have always placed great value on a person's name and reputation and worked hard to keep mine above reproach, so hearing about these character assassinations was quite upsetting. They hurt deeply, but it was even more hurtful to find that they had been believed by those who knew me. I wondered just how many others believed them as well. In their defense, however, I also knew firsthand how convincing and persuasive Cat could be.

As our conversation progressed, it became all too obvious what had really been stolen: seven years of our relationship. The painful truth of this reality settled over the four of us, bringing with it tears and a sense of loss. Drying their eyes, John and Stacie confessed that they were initially surprised that we had agreed to meet with them. They were told that I would never allow Sandy to speak with or see any family member. Sandy was depicted as zombie, a mindless puppet, and I, the master puppeteer.

They went on to share that I became un-affectionately referred to as the "Jerk." I consider myself a pretty likable guy, but the picture Cat painted depicted me as a real creep. Though I was excited about the opportunity to set the record straight, it would take me some time to fully process through the emotions from old wounds that were reopened.

SANDY

Our meal was finished, our shared desert devoured, and our coffee had long grown cold when our server explained that the restaurant was closing. Reluctant to end our time, we all stood and warmly embraced. John and Stacie vowed to never again believe something that was said without first checking out the facts; we did the same. Apologies poured from their hearts. Forgiveness flowed from ours. Together, the two streams—one of regret and the other of release—merged into a healing river of God's love, evident through our tears. Drying our eyes, we all promised to get our children together as soon as possible. They needed the connection with their relatives. Family is important.

The Lord worked a miracle of healing that evening. Relationships were restored and Scott was vindicated. Nonetheless, it troubled me deeply that this man who had so willingly sacrificed himself and all he had worked for to care for me was being portrayed as the perpetrator of an assortment of crimes and misdeeds. My heart swelled with love for my husband, who could have reacted to these accusations. Instead, he chose to set aside his painful feelings in order to listen to and understand the deception that had clouded the eyes of my loved ones. He then ultimately went beyond this and forgave. What a night to remember!

SCOTT

It was disturbing to discover that though we no longer had direct contact with Cat, our lives continued to be impacted by this individual. I was appalled at the lengths Cat was willing to go in order to bring me down and destroy my reputation. Little did I know how far Cat had already traveled…

"What do you mean Cat has been taking pictures of us?" I asked Sandy, my emotionally-charged words exposing the concern that swept over me at the violation and astonishment of it all.

"I don't know," Sandy replied. "All I know is what John told me. He said Cat purchased a camera with a telephoto lens and has been taking pictures of us. John called me as soon as he saw recent pictures of us that Cat claimed to have taken while parked down the street from our house."

"You've got to be kidding! Why would Cat be taking pictures of us, and why haven't we noticed Cat in the neighborhood?" I asked.

"John said Cat is driving a new car and sporting a disguise. I don't know why Cat is taking these photos. But then, why does Cat do half the things Cat does?" Sandy sighed in frustration. "I don't understand why Cat doesn't just leave us alone! It feels like we are being stalked!" Her resignation lifted, replaced by righteous indignation. "Maybe we should report this to the police. We have evidence with these pictures. Maybe it's time we pursue legal action again."

This new revelation left us a little shaken. We considered calling the police but decided against it, wondering just how illegal it was to take photos while sitting on a city street. We did not want to worry the boys, who were now twelve, fourteen, and fifteen, but we felt they needed to know, possibly for their own safety. When they returned home from school that afternoon we sat down and told them what we had learned. It was comforting to see their responses; they no longer feared Cat. On the contrary, we had to caution them to use restraint, as they were prepared to flex their growing muscles and physically defend themselves. After everyone had fully expressed their feelings, the five of us prayed together for wisdom, awareness, and for continued covering and protection.

After our sons went to bed that evening, Sandy and I stayed up praying and discussing our recent discovery. In the interest of sleep, we decided to call it a night. Sandy went off to bed, while I felt compelled to check the doors one last time. Opening the blinds covering the front window, I half expected to find a strange car parked in front of our house. I was more than ready for, even welcoming of, a confrontation with Cat. The empty street was almost a disappointment. Closing the blinds, I went to check in on our sons once again. After assuring myself they were okay, I headed for my office at the other end of the house. I still needed to turn off my aquarium light.

Upon entering my private domain, I dropped, exhausted, into my sturdy desk chair and sighed. As I slowly reached to extinguish the light, I was temporarily distracted by the brilliant colors and fluid movements of my aquatic pets. As I watched the bright blues, vibrant oranges, and deep reds flit back and forth, disturbing images of our strange experiences darted through my mind: the hang-up calls, the beheaded sparrows, the disemboweled rabbit, the stolen recordings of Sandy's sessions, my car tampered with at work, and the demonic manifestations and attacks. It all seemed too coincidental. Now, with our new findings added to the mix, I found it even more unsettling. *There was evidence that Cat was behind all of this, but Cat certainly could not have acted alone. What type of people could Cat be connected with? What is really going on here?*

My troubling thoughts gave way to anger as I considered the abuse my boys had endured. Vivid memories assaulted me as I recalled the day they told us how Cat terrorized them with stories of bloodthirsty werewolves who would rip them apart if they ever told their secrets. I cringed as I thought of them being shown Cat's gun collection and the warning that Cat would shoot them if they ever told.

Anger slowly gave way to guilt and a sense of powerlessness at not being able to protect my sons from these horrible experiences. These feelings were not new; they had reared their ugly heads many times before. Fatigue began to get the better of me, but my mind refused to give in until it could piece this mysterious puzzle together. What was Cat up to now? What was Cat truly capable of? My sleepy mind wondered, *Have we simply been lulled into the illusion that things are finally okay? Are we being stalked? Are we in danger? Would Cat actually try to make good on those threats?*

My thoughts began to trail off when I was startled by a noise that broke the silence of our sleeping house. *Everyone is in bed; what is that noise?* As I walked to the bedrooms to investigate, I attempted to calm myself with the reassurance that it was probably just our son getting dressed in his sleep again.

Heading into the hallway, I noticed that his bedroom door was closed; it had been opened the last time I checked. A sliver of light escaped from underneath. As I approached the door, I heard an eerie, demonic-like voice coming from his room. It was muffled by the closed door, yet the words were clear: "I warned you what would happen if you talked!" Adrenaline raced through my veins as raw terror and a protective rage overtook me. Kicking the door open, I burst into the room to find a werewolf pointing a shotgun at my son. The terror in my child's eyes was paralyzing.

Startled at my presence, the figure quickly turned in my direction, training the gun on me. Reacting out of pure instinct, I pushed the barrel of the shotgun away from me, and not a second too soon. A shot fired, followed by a deafening roar as the shell exploded into the wall behind me. I could hear Sandy's screams over the ringing in my ears. I wrestled our unknown assailant to the ground, attempting to wrench the gun free. My hands recoiled; the heat from the gun barrel burned, causing me to lose the advantage. As we continued to wrestle, I was amazed at the strength of this being, its power fueled by raw hatred and rage. The werewolf disguise looked frighteningly real and effectively portrayed the murderous intent of whatever soul lurked beneath. The realistic feel of the fur as we struggled only added to its lifelike terror. The battle raged. We grappled, slamming each other against walls and furniture alike. I was determined not to let our attacker fire off another round from the gun it clutched in a vice-like grip. Grunts, snarling, and cursing could be heard in the midst of the struggle. The back of my skull collided with the top of the desk, yet I maintained a stranglehold I'd managed to secure around the creature's neck as I began my fall. My head throbbed and I saw stars, but I had the attacker firmly in my grasp. Out of my periphery, I noticed Sandy seizing the moment to run in and rescue our terrified son from his hiding place under the bed. Gathering him up, she rushed him back to the door, where his brothers stood waiting to pull them both to safety.

Rolling myself atop the vial intruder, I pinned it to the floor. With blind determination I reached down, grabbed a handful of hair, and in one harsh tug ripped off the ungodly mask. I was astonished by the familiar face that leered up at me. "You!" I screamed. Recognition hit me like a blast from the menacing gun. With a sickening smirk of satisfaction, Cat glared up at me. Surprise and rage rocketed by an overdose of adrenalin slammed into me, sending me staggering back. "What are you doing in my house?" I screamed.

Ignoring my question, Cat seized the opportunity of my obvious distraction and kneed me in the groin, dropping me to the ground, doubled over in pain. Freed from my grasp, Cat reclaimed the gun and took aim at my chest. Screams and shouts from my family in the hall urged me forward. With swiftness I did not know I possessed, I pushed through the pain and somehow managed to kick the gun free before a shot could be fired. Diving for the gun, I was stopped short by a sharp stabbing throb in my thigh. I looked down to see the handle of a small knife protruding from my leg. Stunned by the immense agony, I instinctively grabbed at my wound. Shrieks and cries from Sandy and the boys brought me out of my pain-induced stupor, making me acutely aware of the impending danger to myself and my family. Willing my pain aside, I regained my senses just in time to see Cat reaching for the shotgun. To my right, I noticed my son's baseball bat. Reaching my hand as far as I could, I willed my fingers to grab hold of the only thing that stood between life and death. Finally securing the weapon, I struggled to stand. As I steadied myself on my one good leg, Cat regained possession of the shotgun.

"I hate you!" Cat snarled through clenched teeth. A malevolent loathing dripped from each word. "You ruined everything, and for that you will pay dearly! You will lose what is most precious to you. Accept the fact that you will never be rid of me. You will always live in fear of what I may do next!"

With that, Cat turned the gun and aimed it at my family, who stood in the doorway, watching on in horror. In that moment I had no doubt that Cat intended to kill them. I glared Cat down and screamed, "You will never harm my wife or my children ever again! It ends here!" Fueled by a protective rage, I took aim and swung as hard as I could.

"Scott... Scott..." Sandy's voice broke through the haze, startling me. "Honey, are you coming to bed?"

"Oh... yeah, I'll be right there," I said, trying to still the adrenalin that coursed through my veins. "I was just sitting here looking at my fish and thinking about Cat. I guess I let my thoughts get away from me," I explained, minimizing all I had just done to protect my family. I was too embarrassed to share the epic battle with Sandy at this moment; the encounter was still all too real to me.

# SURVIVAL SKILL

# *Tell Yourself What's True*

> Summing it all up, friends, I'd say you'll do best by filling your minds and meditating on things true.
>
> Philippians 4:8 MSG

SCOTT

Would our nightmare ever end? It began to feel as though no matter what we did, we would never be free. Even a physical move to an undisclosed location didn't change anything. Like a lurking shadow, our past followed us everywhere we went. Was there was no escape?

Discovering that Cat had been spying on us was the last straw for me. I was outraged at this invasion of our privacy. Frustration that our family would never be free of the grief this person brought into our lives and exasperation that I had been helpless to stop it fueled my mind's epic battle with Cat. This semi-conscious daydream, although a bit cathartic, did nothing to actually solve our problems or change our situation. It was not real, nor was it true.

## The Danger of *Stories*

SCOTT AND SANDY

When we are not telling ourselves what is true, we are in essence, telling ourselves stories. By *stories,* we do not mean a life story, such as our account we share in this book. Instead, for our purposes, we define stories as interpretations of one's experiences that are based in assumptions rather than cold, hard facts. Though they may contain an element of truth, they are conjecture and fabrications we create in order to fill in the blanks when we don't, or can't, obtain the necessary facts. Since these creative conclusions are not necessarily 100 percent true or representative of the actual events themselves or the real intentions of others, they are stories.

What makes stories dangerous is the false reality they create. Because our stories can be quite compelling and believable, we typically don't recognize them as false and therefore, we believe them to be true. This false reality creates an illusion that feels very real. For example: have you ever been stopped at a traffic light when the person beside you shifts into reverse and travels backward? Suddenly, you find yourself desperately stomping on your brakes to avoid rolling into the intersection and the path of oncoming traffic. The backward motion of the other car gives you the illusion that you are moving forward when, in fact, you remain stopped. After a moment of panic, you realize the reality of your situation. You were never moving—the other car was! Finally, your heart ceases its pounding and you begin to feel both relieved and silly. Yet your mind continues its struggle to reconcile the fact that the experience seemed so real. Similarly, the sensations your stories provide can feel real enough that you automatically accept them as truth. Furthermore, when fueled by intense emotions, stories perpetuate themselves and take on a life of their own.

As we came to understand the concept of stories, we developed our next Survival Skill: *Tell Yourself What's True.* Though the idea of being truthful with oneself was not a new concept for us, looking at truth from the perspective of how we can tell ourselves stories was.

We soon discovered several stories we had not only developed but bought into. These stories prevented us from moving forward by burdening us with much unnecessary anxiety, depression, frustration, and anger. Eliminating them in the interest of truth was a significant turning point in our journey.

## *Scott's Stories*

Even though Sandy was doing much better, the stress of caring for her and the boys over an extended period of time had taken its toll, leaving me feeling very uncared for. Also, due to the nature of Sandy's abuse, the intimacy aspect of our marriage had become a problem for her, translating into a problem for me as well. I had pushed aside many of my personal feelings and needs in the interest of caring for my family. However, these feelings would no longer be ignored, and I found myself unable to continue to hold back their rising tide of resentment.

The extent of Sandy's past trauma and the severity of her emotional and mental break made her progress often laborious and uncertain. Dr. Morrison's warning "Scott, you need to prepare yourself. Sandy may never be the same again" continued to torment me. Fears and beliefs that Sandy and our situation would never improve eventually scripted themselves into several full-blown stories:

- *Sandy will never be completely well.*
- *Our struggle will never change, and I will have to suffer for the rest of my life.*
- *I will never have my wife back; never again will I experience the marriage I desire, and my needs will never be met.*

Each time my stories replayed themselves, I became more convinced of their reality. The more I bought into their lies, the more depressed and hopeless I became and the deeper the chasm grew between Sandy and me. As a result, I had to work harder to maintain our connection.

Once I became aware that I was telling myself stories, and of the dangers they presented, I made a conscious decision to no longer buy into these untruths. Instead, I began to critically challenge my thoughts and search for what was actually true. In this process I found it helpful to separate the parts of my stories that were true, and therefore real, from those that were not.

*Sandy will never be completely well:* Yes, it was true that Sandy still had progress to make in her recovery process. But did this guarantee that she would never be completely well? Was I able to gaze into the future and know with absolute certainly that this was true? No. Yet I might as well have had that advanced insight, because this despairing belief had become my reality. Though our situation was admittedly frustrating, my story caused me to suffer needlessly with an exaggerated hopelessness. Putting my feelings aside, I had to admit she really had made a great deal of progress in a relatively short period of time, considering the extent of her breakdown. It was actually pretty amazing that she was doing as well as she was.

*Our struggle will never change, and I will have to suffer for the rest of my life:* With all the changes that had already occurred, there was no reason to believe that Sandy's recovery would not continue. Yet my story had the potential to actually sabotage her progress and keep me miserable and stuck.

*I will never have my wife back; never again will I experience the marriage I desire, and my needs will never be met:* It was true that my needs were not being met. This was a very real fact that left me feeling unloved, sad, lonely, and at times, even angry. But did it mean that things would never change and that my needs would never again be met? Not necessarily. Did it feel this way? Yes. Did I fear that this might actually happen? Most certainly! I felt this way not because it was true, but rather, because I believed it to be true. My story took what was possible and made it a reality. And as long as I told myself this, I would continue to experience more unnecessary pain, turmoil, and defeat than our situation warranted. I was living life as though my worst fears had already happened. It was in this process that I realized a great truth: just because something feels real doesn't make it true.

When I allowed my stories to influence my thoughts and behaviors, I only confused and worsened my situation. However, as I challenged and released my stories, I opened the door for positive changes and improvements in my life and in Sandy's as well. I also gained a new perspective and discovered that things weren't as bad as they appeared and felt. It became all too clear that much of my unrelenting emotional torment came more from the pain that my stories produced than from actual events themselves.

Just because something feels real doesn't make it true.

## *Sandy's Stories*

I had my fair share of stories as well. Like Scott's, most of them were centered on our struggle with my mental and emotional health. I believed that I was somehow defective because of my past abuse. Even when I felt strong and confident, there was always a lingering doubt. I felt as though I had a big C for Crazy emblazoned on my forehead for all to see. After all, how could anyone take me seriously now that I'd had a mental breakdown and spent years recovering? I believed that no matter what I did, I would always be looked at as the pitiful woman who suffered from mental problems.

When I was feeling depressed or anxious, I would become exasperated, believing I would never get better. This belief soon evolved into another that said, "I need to stay ill, because if I am healthy, others will expect more out of me than I can accommodate." This line of thinking kept me a victim to my disability.

I had other stories that included Scott and our sons. With the loss of extended family, I believed a lie that my own family would grow up and desert me. This is why I had such fear of conflict. If I could just keep everyone happy, our family would stay close. With regards to Scott, I believed I could never please him in the areas that really mattered. Every area in which I struggled was an area of significance to him. I felt I could never win.

Basically, my stories went like this:

- *People won't take me seriously because I am defective.*
- *People view me as crazy.*
- *I will never be mentally healthy.*
- *I cannot be physically healthy because I cannot keep up with the expectations of others.*
- *I will lose my kids if I engage in any conflict with them.*
- *I can never please Scott no matter what I do.*

These stories were invasive and encompassed nearly every area of my life. As long as I believed my stories, my progress would be stymied. The novels that played out in my mind held me back from my full potential; they kept me ineffective as a woman, wife, and mother, and a victim to my past. How could I compete with these beliefs? I had a story standing against every area in which I desired to succeed. The reality was I couldn't. The answer was not found in competing with my stories. Rather, it was in finding and adhering to what was really true.

I broke down my stories so I could closely examine them:

*People won't take me seriously because I'm defective. People view me as crazy:* Is that really true? Sure, it feels true. But is it really true? Do I have evidence that this is how people actually view me? No, not really. What real evidence do I have? Actually, people treat me no differently from anyone else and actually seem to respect what I have to say. So maybe my belief is not actually true but something I feel about myself. What would happen if I chose to see myself in the same light others see me? What if I saw myself as whole and okay as opposed to defective?

*I will never be mentally healthy. I cannot be physically healthy because I cannot keep up with the expectations of others:* Is that true? Although it often felt real and did have some basis in truth, it was not true. Yes, I'd had a breakdown and yes, I had chronic fatigue syndrome, but that did not mean my life was controlled and dictated by these two realities. In fact, I had come a long way from that fateful day of the breakdown, and the more mentally healthy I became, the more my physical health recovered. I also realized it was not truly the expectations of others I feared, but my own. These frightened me because I did not feel I had the physical ability to accomplish all I wanted. However, I came to understand that God would not put me in a place if I was not ready. As the popular quote from an unknown author goes, "The will of God will not take me where the grace of God cannot protect me." I needed to trust him and stop projecting my fear into the future. God will sustain me in whatever it is he wants for me.

*I will lose my kids if I engage in any conflict with them. I can never please Scott no matter what I do:* These two stories impacted me the most. My family meant the world to me, and the thought of losing any of them was too painful to imagine. Nonetheless, I faced these stories head on. Was it true that our sons would forsake our relationship? Was it really true that I could do nothing to please Scott? After sorting through these painful questions, I realized that I did not have evidence that either of them was entirely true. Our family was close, and though the boys often fought, they cared for each other and loved and respected us, even when we confronted them. The closeness of our family was apparent; the evidence of such devotion far outweighed any evidence to the contrary. It was simply my fear that reinforced my story and my story compounded my fear.

What about Scott? Was it true that I could never please him? Sadly, there were areas affected by my past trauma, but there were many other areas where our love flowed easily and generously. By recognizing this truth, I was better able to move on with my recovery. The more healing I received, the more I focused on being grounded in the present moment and the less my past had the opportunity to infiltrate and infect it. All the work I engaged in eventually invited more intimacy into our marriage. Sure, things could have been better, but given our circumstances, life was pretty good. We discovered that as we both worked to eliminate our stories, we began to experience the marriage we each longed for.

As you can see, each of our stories contained an element of truth, but that truth was then skewed by our own interpretation and assumptions. If we had continued in our stories, our lives and relationship would be very different today. Our self-fulfilling prophesies might have come true. Scott might have left in search of someone who could meet his needs (as many choose to do), the boys might have been pushed away because of my fear, and I might have been re-hospitalized, convinced that I was crazy. These alternate outcomes are speculations, of course; nonetheless, the mind is a very powerful tool. Without our contesting our stories, who knows where they could have carried us?

## The Importance of Truth

SCOTT AND SANDY

What you tell yourself about your struggles greatly impacts your ability to move past them. This is due to the fact that, true or not, whatever you tell yourself becomes your reality. For example, if you do not believe you can overcome your troubles, chances are you might not. If you truly believe that things will never get any better, they probably won't. The reason these self-fulfilling prophesies play themselves out is not because they are true, but rather, because you've convinced yourself they are. As a result, they have become your reality. These self-statements might as well be true because they feel true and appear real.

You may not always believe what others tell you, but
you will always believe what you tell yourself.

Obviously, therefore, it stands to reason that only by telling yourself what's true can you effectively improve or change your circumstances. God felt it important enough to repeatedly encourage us throughout Scripture to think on and further tell ourselves only those things which are true.

---

## IT'S YOUR TURN

We invite you to peer into the depths of your own inner thoughts and see if you recognize any of your own stories. Some may jump right out at you, while others will be much more subtle.

## Storytelling

We are commonly asked, "How can I know when or if I'm telling myself stories?" One thing is for sure: we cannot rely on our feelings to identify stories. After all, how does a story feel?

It feels real—very real! There are, however, several clues that scream *story.* For instance, when your thoughts contain absolutes such as "always" or "never," you can pretty much bet that some degree of storytelling is taking place. Reacting and over-exaggerating are also strong indicators that a story is engaged. We have compiled a list of clues to help you identify when you may be in storytelling mode. Take a moment and familiarize yourself with it.

Storytelling clues:

- Using absolutes like "always" and "never."
- Overreacting.
- Feeling defeated and hopeless.
- Nursing hurts.
- Over-exaggerating and "awfulizing" the situation.
- Interpreting a situation from an all-or-nothing/black-or-white perspective.
- Basing the truth on feelings.
- Believing a situation will never change.

We have also provided you with a list of common stories as an additional aid to help you identify when you are telling yourself stories. Look the list over and see if any apply to you.

Common Stories:

- There is nothing I can do to change X.
- I will have to suffer with X forever.
- No matter what I do, I will never please X.
- I will never get over X.
- Things are so bad that they will never change or improve.

- If God really loved me, he wouldn't have allowed me to experience X.
- My needs will never be met.
- I am a failure.
- God does not/will not accept me.
- If it wasn't for X, I wouldn't be in this position.
- God is punishing me.
- I am unworthy.

Did you identify with any of these stories? If so, relax. It simply means that you are human, after all. The truth is: we all tell ourselves stories to one degree or another, especially when we are suffering some sort of setback or letdown. This is because we all have an innate need to make sense of our experiences. However, it is important to not allow this to become an excuse to tell ourselves stories.

## Truth Telling

This next section is dedicated to helping you indentify, challenge, and ultimately rid yourself of your stories. One of the ways to make certain you're not telling a story is to ensure that you're telling yourself the truth.

### *Challenge Your Thoughts*

Begin by challenging your thoughts instead of taking them at face value. Hold your inner conversations accountable by challenging them to determine if what you are telling yourself is true. Consciously sifting through your thought life and searching for and expelling any non-truths is an important step in overcoming your struggles.

Challenge your self-talk by holding your thoughts under the scrutiny of the truth. Ask yourself the following questions:

- What am I telling myself?
- Is what I'm telling myself really true?
- How do I know that it's true?
- Do I have 100 percent certainty that this is true?
- What evidence do I have that this is true?
- Could I be making an assumption?
- What else might be true instead? What are some other possibilities?

As you consider these questions, be brutally honest no matter what your feelings are telling you. It is important to realize that a thought isn't true simply because it feels real. When asked with intention and honesty, these questions will help you identify your stories and will prevent you from creating new ones. They will further ensure that you consistently tell yourself the truth.

## *Let go of your Stories*

While challenging your thoughts, did you identify any possible story? Are you ready to take the next step and begin liberating yourself from that story? The choice is up to you. Letting go of your stories can be difficult and even scary. Like old friends, they are familiar and often provide a level of comfort. However, as with negative influences, they are toxic. Be okay with the discomfort that may result from releasing these old yet destructive associates. It's a normal part of the process.

Perhaps it would be helpful to remind yourself of the consequences of keeping your stories. First of all, they will only bring pain and destruction into your life. They will sabotage your ability to change or improve your circumstances. Furthermore, your stories will imprison you within your struggles, intensifying and exaggerating your pain, as they did in our lives.

## *Replace Your Story with What's Really True*

If your story is not true, how you can know what is true? Begin by asking God to help you be open to the truth. Then look for the alternate possibilities. For instance, what would the opposite of your story be? If your story entails another person, try giving them the benefit of the doubt. Or better yet, start asking rather than assuming. Think outside the box. Seek out a fresh perspective and ask someone who is neutral and objective to help you determine what is really true.

Once you have arrived at the truth, actively replace your story with this new truth. Write it down on paper. Repeat it out loud. Share it with someone. Allow your mind to make a shift in the way it previously viewed your experiences to what is true and real.

## *Remove Any Story Reinforcers*

Replacing your story with the truth, though essential, is not enough to keep it from returning. You will also need to remove any story reinforcers. Story reinforcers consist of anything that continues to fortify, rather than challenge, your story. For instance, every time you revisit or re-tell your story, you reinforce it. As the old saying goes, "A tale grows taller each time it's told." So each time you re-tell it and re-feel your story, the bigger, more painful, and more entrenched it becomes. Stop re-telling your story, even to yourself.

If your reinforcers are people, you may consider changing or limiting time with certain acquaintances. Seek out healthy, objective, supportive (not enabling) relationships with people who will tell you openly, honestly, and lovingly the truth you need to hear.

Identify anything in your life that may be reinforcing any stories you are working to eliminate. As much as possible, rid them from your life.

### *Gather New Evidence*

A story requires supporting evidence to sustain itself and will continually seek out verification, even if it has to invent it. Meanwhile, any evidence that contradicts the story is conveniently overlooked. Left unchallenged and uncontested, these stories will continue to grow and develop all of the intricacy and detail of a full-length novel, the script by which your life will be directed.

Thoroughly eliminating your stories requires you to discredit and discard your old evidence. Additionally, intentionally look for and mentally record new evidence to support the truth. It may help you to write down this new evidence. Be vigilant and relentless. At the same time, watch for the old evidence to pop up again, trying to regain a foothold. Resist it immediately and allow it no place in your thoughts.

## CONCLUSION

SANDY

Identifying and releasing our stories can be challenging and, as we've stated, even a bit scary. I can still recall the first time I handled a confrontation between Scott and one of our sons while choosing to release my story that this conflict would mean an end to our relationship. Well, I didn't exactly handle the confrontation; actually, that was the point. In the past I would panic any time my radar-like antenna picked up even the slightest hint of conflict or disagreement. Acting quickly, I'd soothe all disgruntled feelings, once again making the world a safe place for all, especially me.

However, this day I determined to look for new evidence to support the truth that a simple conflict would not result in the destruction of my family. It was no easy task to stand by and listen to my loved ones' raised voices in a heated discussion. Everything within me screamed for me to jump in and end the discomfort, but I was set on giving the truth a try. My discomfort grew to the point that I had to leave, retreating to my bedroom and shutting the door.

Now, just so you don't get the wrong idea, neither Scott nor our sons are the aggressive type. Even though from my perspective it sounds like a knock-down-drag-out, it was nothing of the sort, just a concerned and loving father laying down the law with his teenaged son in need of direction.

When the dust settled, I crawled from my hiding place with my hand securely across my mouth, metaphorically speaking, of course. I found father and son standing in the middle of the family room in a warm, loving embrace. I was amazed! They had worked out their differences and no one was bleeding, no one had stormed out vowing to never return. As a matter of fact, their love and respect for each other seemed to have grown. I hated to admit it, but they handled it better without me. That totally went against my story. How could that be possible? Well… it was. The truth won out over the story I had believed. I now had new evidence I could employ when the next confrontation hit. My story was on its way out the door!

## SCOTT AND SANDY

Now, armed with the understanding of stories and the destruction they bring into your life, you too have a choice to make. You can determine to tell yourself what's true regarding your painful circumstances, or you can choose to hold onto your stories. If you opt for truth, your reality will be true, healthy, and forward moving. If, however, you opt for stories, you will continue to suffer the consequences of such tales because your reality will remain skewed and false. More than likely, you will be stuck in the unnecessary pain, turmoil, and defeat you already feel and you will unwittingly sabotage your progress.

We urge you to avoid becoming the author of your own self-deception and self-destruction. Telling yourself what's true has the power to set you free. It has provided such liberty in our lives; we know it will for you. But, as with all the survival skills, the choice to implement it is yours.

# *Lessons Learned*

SCOTT AND SANDY

It was 1998, and we'd left our home church to help a pastor friend start a new church. He too had a heart for people who were hurting, and he focused his ministry around helping such individuals. Our own business (run with a ministry mindset) dovetailed nicely with his ministry. Through our collaboration, many were receiving the help they needed.

Meanwhile, our financial saga continued and we were losing the battle.

SANDY

"I tell you what: if anyone deserves a break, it's you guys. I can't believe all you've been through. God is going to turn everything around and return all that you've lost!"

It felt good to be championed by such a godly and highly respected friend as Pastor Ray.

"In Joel 2:25," Ray continued, "God says he's going to repay the years the locusts have eaten. I just can't help but believe that he's is going to do the same for you."

God's words, spoken through Ray, were like cool, refreshing water to our dehydrated and shriveled spirits. Our hearts hungered to believe that this prophetic passage would extend to us. Ray's biblical analogy was certainly appropriate; our lives indeed resembled a field ravaged by the invasive insects. Like devastated farmers, nothing we did seemed to make any difference. It had been seven long years of emotional and financial struggle, and we were exhausted. We longed to be rescued from this perpetual swarm, to have God step in and both right the wrongs and replenish our decimated finances.

God granted our deepest desire in answering our prayers for emotional healing. However, this didn't miraculously and instantaneously happen. It was a process, and one that required much hard work on all our parts. But it was an answered prayer, nonetheless. In this aspect, our futures looked bright. However, it was now our financial situation and our losses that weighed heavily on our hearts and minds.

Relaxing in his favorite chair after a satisfying Sunday dinner, Scott drowsily pondered Ray's encouraging proclamation. "Did it seem to you as though God was speaking directly to us when Ray shared that verse?" Scott asked.

"Yeah, it did feel that way to me," I responded from the kitchen just a few feet away. My little mop of a Lhasa Apso puppy, Sophie, played happily underfoot. "It also made me feel special, like God was showing us he cares about all we've been through. Maybe things are going to finally turn around."

Finishing up the last of the dishes, I turned to join Scott, with Sophie in her established place at my heels. As I stepped into our newly constructed family room, my heart swelled with pride at our accomplishment. I still could not believe that the five of us, with the help of a friend, had actually built this much-needed addition. While Scott contemplated our message from

God, I gazed at our handiwork as I lounged on the couch with Sophie curled up by my side.

I thought fondly about Jack, our friend who'd used his solid financial influence and good name to help us procure funding from the bank in the form of a refinance. If it weren't for Jack, we wouldn't be enjoying this room today. We were considered a high risk in the eyes of the lending institution.

We had drawn up our own plans and gotten the necessary permits for this expansion that spanned the entire back of the house. Our project turned our cramped 1,100 square foot home into a comfortable and spacious 2,000 square feet. This extra space provided us with a larger master bedroom and relocated one of our son's rooms, which in turn opened up space for a dining area and offered us a sizeable family room as well. We'd needed to do something, and moving again was out of the question. There simply wasn't enough room for the five of us, especially as the boys grew older. At twelve, fourteen, and fifteen, their growing bodies and changing needs required more space. With the addition, our home now felt like a comfy, roomy slipper and no longer like a tight, pinching shoe two sizes too small.

Today we were finally taking full advantage of its cozy comfort. Our home was tranquil and quiet after our sons deserted us in favor of their friends.

"Hey, honey?"

"Hmm," Scott murmured from his food-induced coma.

"I was thinking a little more about what Ray said this morning, and ... well, you know how we've been hearing a lot lately about how God is going to bless us?"

"Uh-huh," he hummed sleepily.

Afraid that I was going to lose him to a nap, I quickly continued. "Well, just the other day my friend Joan said God has big plans for us but that we first need to step out in faith and start living as if we already had what we need. Then, she said, God will come through and bless us. Maybe she's right. After all, you've been working diligently for such a long time, and yet we can't seem to get ahead. I wonder if God is waiting for us to step out first. Maybe he wants us to live as though we already have what we long for and once we do step out, his blessings will follow?"

"I'm not sure." Scott yawned and stretched. "I know we've been hearing that, but I'm not convinced that's the way it works." Sitting up, he continued. "We know that when we're faithful in the little things God will bless us with more. But I have to admit, it does feel like we've been faithful for a long time without much in return. It is frustrating, that's for sure." Scott looked over at me for a moment. "I know that look; what's going on in that head of yours?"

I grinned and picked up my sleeping pup as I sat up. "It would be nice to have some furniture for this new room."

"What do you think we're sitting on now?" Scott said with that characteristic mischievous grin he often flashed when I tried to be serious.

"Ha ha, very funny. But really, honey, this garage sale set wasn't in the greatest condition when we bought it seven years ago. Besides, there's barely enough room for the five of us to sit with the boys getting bigger. A couch and a chair just won't cut it anymore." I paused for a moment before continuing, "Honey, it's embarrassing when we have company." I stopped myself as my frustration began to get the better of me. Irritations and disappointment with the years of hardship were demanding to be heard. We had been working hard to make ends meet, yet the ends rarely ever connected.

In response to our fiscal imbalance, over the years we'd found creative ways to generate money. With the help of our sons, we raised and sold fancy rabbits, having over sixty breeders at one time. Though counseling full time, Scott also painted houses when the opportunity arose, and I periodically took on transcribing work from home. These additional enterprises generated supplementary income, though it was still not enough to support our growing family of five and cover our past and present medical debt. What extra money we did generate created a tradeoff; it disqualified me from my disability benefits. This meant the loss of extra capital and, more importantly, the termination of our health insurance benefits. Affordable health coverage was difficult to secure due to our family's now preexisting medical conditions and Scott's self-employment status. But we'd learned the hard way the risk involved in not having adequate coverage. To compensate, we lived on a very restricted, no-frills budget.

Somewhat successful in my attempts to calm my frustrations, I pressed on. "Honey, you know that I try not to complain, but it's becoming more and more difficult to remain positive. It's been over seven years since you had to sell many of our belongings to pay my hospital bill. Thank you for doing all you did to keep us afloat during that time. I know it wasn't easy for you. But we still haven't been able to afford to replace most of what we lost. I try to be grateful for what we have, but ... " My words trailed off as I resisted saying what I really felt. But the cry of my heart was too strong to resist, so I continued. " ... the boys are still sleeping on the floor, for Pete's sake! Is it so wrong to want beds for our sons or a dresser for our clothes?" I stopped as my voice began to crack. Sophie, sensing my distress, began tenderly licking my hand.

Scott joined me on the couch, put his arm around me, and waited for me regain my composure. I went on. "Why are we still in this financially barren place? When is God going to tangibly bless us? Something has got to change!"

I waited for Scott to respond, but he seemed lost in his own thoughts. So I continued. "I don't know ... what if God wants us to take the first step and buy some new furnishings? This might be his way of replacing what we've lost. What do you think?" Fighting against the ray of hope that I longed to let shine yet dared not for fear of another letdown, I held my breath and waited for a response.

"I completely agree with you, honey, but I honestly don't know how we can afford it," Scott reluctantly responded. "We are already financially strapped."

SCOTT

The discouragement that clouded my wife's face in that moment nearly broke my heart in two. We'd been through a great deal, and she'd gone without for much of that time. We'd lost nearly everything we had acquired. I know it wasn't easy for her to run our household on what little we had. Not many modern wives have had to pluck and dress their own chickens, for goodness' sakes! She believed in me and supported my career change, even though it meant continued financial hardship while I built a new business. As the provider, I wanted to make her happy. I wanted her to feel satisfied and secure. I felt like I had let her down. How could I say no again?

I took Sandy's hand and tried to explain. "This journey hasn't been easy on either of us, especially you. It really doesn't seem fair. We've been without what most would consider items of necessity for a long time now. Yet, on the practical side, we've avoided 'spending' debt, even though we still have our medical debt. Living frugally and only buying what we can afford has helped us get as far as we have." I sat back, leaning my head against the couch. My attempts to sound encouraging by pointing out the positive side of our situation fell flat, even to my own ears.

Lost in frustration and drowning in disappointment, Sandy despondently dropped her head against the back of the couch.

Desperate to fix Sandy's distress, I allowed my thoughts to take me into uncharted territory. "Maybe … I don't know … "

"What?" Sandy sighed.

"It's just this whole living 'as if' thing. It does get you thinking, doesn't it?"

At the change in my tone, Sandy's face lit up once again. "Hey, I know," she chimed in, "do we have any money left from the refinance?"

"No, we used the last of it to install this carpet," I answered, knowing where she was going with this and hating that I'd squelched her idea.

"Oh." She sighed, the sparkle in her eyes fading.

We sat in silence for several depressing moments. The coziness of the new room had faded, pushed aside by a cold emptiness. Even the dog noticed the chill and wiggled around, seeking her former comfort.

I could no longer take it. I had to do something! Abandoning my common sense for my wife's happiness, I made an unprecedented decision, one that was out of character for me.

I smiled and patted Sandy's knee. "You know what: I don't have clients until early afternoon tomorrow. Let's go look at furniture first thing in the morning and see what we can do."

"Seriously?" Sophie jumped at Sandy's squeal. "But how will we pay for it?"

"The Furniture Warehouse has financing, so I figure we could make payments and trust God to help us. If it is true that he wants us to take a leap of faith, this could be our starting place. And it's not like we would be buying anything that we really didn't need. Everything we've been hearing suggests we make the first move and once we do, God will provide. Like you said, something's got to change; maybe God *is* waiting for us to step out in faith."

Barely containing her excitement, Sandy practically bounced into my lap and gave me a loving, grateful hug. In spite of myself, I couldn't help my boyish grin. It felt so good to see my wife this happy and to consider that God would bless us in such a material, tangible way.

SANDY

I was so overjoyed that I could hardly sleep that night. As I lay awake, I reviewed all the years we had lived in need and lack. "We can't buy this ... We can't do that ... " I was weary from telling ourselves no. Surely God intended to bless us. With all we'd been through, there had to be a silver lining somewhere. Ray and Joan always seemed to hear from the Lord, and their words reflected what many others had said. The more I thought about it, the more convinced I became: we needed to take the first step. It all made perfect sense.

Morning did not come soon enough. After a quick breakfast, we were out the door and on our way. It was so exciting to finally allow ourselves the opportunity to even consider such a purchase.

We pulled into the parking lot of one of the largest furniture stores in the area. Although it was privately owned, they were known for their low prices. I had spent many a Sunday perusing their ads, admiring the lovely furniture yet knowing it was out of our reach.

Walking through the big glass doors, I was immediately captivated by all the beautiful furnishings before me. Having never set foot in a furniture store, this was a big moment for me. Everything we had was either falling apart or simply inadequate for our needs. The sight of the colorful upholstery and the smell of new, polished wood toyed with my senses, bringing on a major attack of the "gimmes": "Gimme one of these" and "Gimme one of those!" Like a child in Willy Wonka's chocolate factory, I was swept up in a dream world. Scott, being the practical one, took my hand and pulled me to the displays of living room furnishings. After all, that's what we came to investigate.

We sat, flopped, and sprawled out on every couch, recliner, and loveseat that called out to us before Scott's sensibility brought us down to earth by pointing out the price tags. Undaunted, I began a quest for the least expensive setup I could find. Gazing across the sea of overstuffed comfort, I spied a hunter green leather sectional. Upon closer inspection I could see it was the perfect size and angle, as though it had been specially made for our long, narrow room. Reaching hesitantly for the tag, I silently prayed this ideal combination sofa, loveseat, end table, and recliner would be affordable. I couldn't believe my eyes. The asking price wasn't terribly bad, and to top it off, it was on sale. What a find! Excitedly, I called for Scott to come have a look, hoping and praying that he too would see the perfection and agree to the purchase. Surely, this was God's plan; it was just too perfect to ignore.

Once Scott finally got there, I gave a performance that rivaled any model from *The Price Is Right.* With flair and flourish, I caressed the sturdy leather, enlightening Scott on its ease of maintenance for even our rough-and-tumble household. Taking Scott's hand, I danced him to the center seat that was set apart by narrow, wooden end table-like pieces, bowing as I invited him to take his throne. Once he was seated, I gracefully lifted the armrest and tripped the hidden lever. His feet were luxuriously swept off the floor, while his body comfortably stretched out as the regal seat reclined. As Scott lounged on the throne, I glided into the seat nearby, and with a wave of my hand, I inconspicuously pressed the button and the end of the loveseat opened, reclining me as well. My demonstration was not yet over. With such grace, I leapt from my repose and sashayed to Scott's side once again. I gently lifted his relaxing arm and for the **pièce de** *résistance,* with an accented "ta da," I flipped the switch. Scott grinned with delight as his body was pulsed and vibrated into a state of relaxation. I felt certain he was hooked.

Reluctantly pulling himself from his massage-induced stupor, Scott gave me the look that said he had mentally calculated the price and concluded it expensive. But he went ahead and asked anyway. "Okay, this thing is amazing, but what's the bottom line? How much is it?" Although I told him the price, he didn't believe it until I showed him the tag. I could see the "Sold" sign alight in his eyes before the word left his mouth. Forgetting all decorum I jumped up and down, clapping in excitement.

I was absolutely giddy at the prospect of this state-of-the-art sectional proudly adorning my new family room. Even Scott could not conceal the exhilaration of having such a luxurious sectional on which to recline each evening. We were both caught up in the excitement of the purchase, so much so that before we knew it, we were heading for the bedroom furnishings.

Surrounded by a plethora of beautifully displayed bedroom suites, we forced ourselves into practicality and sought out three no-nonsense beds for the boys. As we explored options for them, we were seduced by the mesmerizing siren call of the coordinating headboards, night-stands, dressers, and chest of drawers for ourselves. Having never owned such luxuries, we were quickly overcome by the spellbinding call. Soon we were opening drawers, gazing into over-sized mirrors, and, to my delighted surprise, eventually considering prices.

"Honey, this is amazing and wonderful, but isn't this too much?" I asked.

"I figure we might as well get what we need now and go from here. After all, God wants to bless us, right?"

With that, we settled on one of the less expensive yet lovely, light-colored heavy pine bedroom sets. Every piece matched. I was dizzy with exuberance. I was going to have matching bedroom furniture, a luxury I had never previously allowed myself to consider.

Suddenly I was feeling very loved, cared for, and blessed by God. I knew the amassing of material possessions in no way equated love; yet I couldn't help but feel God finally cared for more than just my basic needs. I was also deeply touched that Scott recognized my desires and longed to meet them. I wanted to wrap my arms around him and plant a big kiss. I did just that!

With a gleam in his eye and his characteristic grin in place, Scott led me across the gigantic showroom to the dining room section. I looked at him with expectancy. *Is he thinking what I think he is thinking?*

"Sweetheart, I want you to have a nice dining room set. You've done so well with what little we've had, and I know how much this means to you. I love you!"

Oh my goodness, could my swollen heart take any more? Tears welled, threatening to spill over my cheeks, as I enveloped Scott in another embrace. Hand in hand, we walked through the mass of tables of varying shapes and sizes. We were both soon drawn to the same set. It was a simple, traditional pedestal oak oval that easily expanded to accommodate two extensions, perfect for our current family of five and the eight-plus we would grow to when the boys married. I was tickled pink! Then Scott caught me eyeing the matching china cabinet. I quickly looked away. We had spent too much money already, but Scott went and looked at the price. Just a couple hundred more ... why not?

This was too much to take in. My giddiness was swept away in the sea of comfort and love that washed over me. God really was blessing us! He truly did care for us! I felt as though I was floating on the most peaceful of clouds. Were my feet even touching the floor?

With our shopping expedition finished, we made our way to the cashier. However, just as we rounded the corner, Scott spied a high-backed bench with two drawers beneath it. Immediately, I could see how perfectly it would fit under our front window and wondered if he was picturing that too. Scott inspected the price tag—just one hundred more. No problem. *Thank you, God!* I couldn't believe my home would finally be fully furnished. *God is good!*

Scott had the information slips we'd gathered from each piece we wanted and he handed them to the cashier while asking for a credit application. Giant, hairy moths suddenly invaded my stomach, threatening to whisk away my visions of the beautiful furniture filling our home. Would we qualify for over five thousand dollars worth of credit? Soon, though, Scott was signing the papers, and with a sigh of relief, the moths retreated, swatted away by restored dreams of a full and blessed house.

The first month with our new furniture went by quickly. Each morning as I awoke in our lovely bedroom, I was tickled. Walking into the dining room, I was thrilled. And by the time my eyes landed on our family room sectional, I was simply ecstatic. Wherever I looked, I no longer saw lack or need. Instead, I saw love. I felt cherished and cared for by both my loving God, who was interested in fulfilling my desires, and my devoted husband. He had stepped out of character, spending money we didn't have, to see that we finally had what we needed. My hopes were lifted, and I just knew the tides were changing in our favor!

We realized our first payment was due soon but also trusted that God would handle it. We waited expectantly each day to see how he would provide. Would he send Scott more clients? Would he give me health enough to manage a work schedule? Would he send us an inheritance from some long lost uncle? Or would God use other creative ways to care for our need? After all, nothing is too difficult for him.

It wasn't long before that first bill arrived. Nothing extra had come into our account to help with the payment, but we weren't too concerned. We scraped together enough to pay it and thanked God for the funds that we knew were on the way. "This was just a little test of our faith," we assured ourselves. "God wants to build our trust, so he's just letting us sweat it out for a bit; the money is on its way!"

By the time the second bill arrived, with no additional funding, our resolve began to weaken. Again, we scraped and scratched until we had enough to cover what we owed. Worry started creeping its way into our hearts, but we bravely determined that God was continuing to test our determination to maintain our faith in him. Shoving the unwelcome worry aside, we marched on, steadfast in our conviction, holding tightly to our faith.

No matter how hard we prayed or how intensely we believed, nothing happened. When the third and fourth payments became due, reality set in: God wasn't going to pay for this furniture; we were. But how? My heartstrings snapped a little each month as nothing but bills filled our mailbox. Where I once felt cherished and cared for, now the old familiar feelings of neglect and abandonment crept back in. This new wound cut me deeply, reaching into the depths of my past abuse. *God wasn't there to protect and help me as a child, and he's clearly not interested in helping us now.*

Scott and I spent many hours praying together. This new pain resurrected old rejections for us both. What began as a symbol of God's restoration, a tangible representation of all that was taken from us—innocence, hope, safety, identity, stability, material possessions, and financial security—became a slap in the face. By not providing payment, God was essentially saying he did not care. At least that was how we interpreted it.

SCOTT

Sandy and I were reading in bed when she could no longer contain her disappointment. "This is so unfair!" she cried, slamming down her book, allowing her pent-up feelings their escape. "No one should have to go through all that we have gone through; no one!" She grabbed a Kleenex and twisted it in her hands. "We've accepted what happened to us and made the best of it. When others would have given up, we hung in there. We've worked hard and done whatever was necessary to help the boys through their trauma, and I've been diligent with my own recovery. Scott, we've done everything God has asked of us. We have served and obeyed him through it all. Even when my healing from chronic fatigue, for which we diligently prayed, didn't come, never once did I get angry at God. We haven't given up and thrown in the towel. But now I'm really tempted to! Even Job was rewarded at the end of his suffering," Sandy continued. "What more could God want from us?"

I reached over, pulled her close, and let her vent while I quietly fought back my own anger and despair.

"How much more are we supposed to take?" Sandy continued. Her body began to tremble as sobs overtook her. "This is too much! I can't take anymore letdowns. When will it stop? We have lost so much. I don't even feel God loves us anymore." I held her until the last wave of torrential tears subsided.

Sandy moved away to blow her nose then snuggled back into my arms to continue. "Will life always be this difficult? Will things ever turn around? Is it asking too much to just catch a break?"

As I listened to Sandy's painful narrative of the last seven-plus years, I found myself fighting to contain my own disappointment and frustration. In spite of my best efforts to resist them, warm tears escaped and began a trail down my own cheeks. She was right. We had been through much and had lost a great deal. We prayed, not only for the replacement of our lost possessions, but also for Sandy's physical healing. Yet nothing happened! Nothing changed! In our desperation, we prayed harder and believed with an even greater faith. But still nothing happened. Though we beat on heaven's door, it was as though no one was home. I felt totally defeated. Inside, I knew that God had a good reason for not answering our prayers as we desired, but I was tired of pacifying myself with good reasons. I wanted things to change. I wanted us to live a normal life.

Suddenly, I was overwhelmed by a painful past that I had worked so diligently to put behind me. The pain and disappointment of it all was too great. The emotional sediment that had finally settled was stirred up once again. Its debris clouded my thoughts, contaminating my sense of well-being. I felt incredibly sad, alone, rejected, uncared for, and angry—really, really angry!

That night, neither of us slept well. My body lay silent while my thoughts raged. The frustration over our situation and the seeming lack of intervention from God gnawed away at the recesses of both of our minds. The next morning, neither of us was ready to jump out of bed. It being a Saturday, we were able to linger for a while. The previous night's dark cloud of hopelessness hung ominously in the air as we laid in silent contemplation.

Feeling compelled to do something to move us out of our hopeless position, I broke the silence and assertively announced, "If God isn't going to help us, then we'll just help ourselves. I'm sick and tired of feeling this way!"

This was the last straw. We had been kicked to the curb one time too many. I'd had enough! We both were angry—angry with God and angry with Cat for starting this whole mess in the first place. How much might we have today had everything not been taken from us?

With a huff, I threw off the blanket and hopped to the floor, the sudden surge of angry adrenalin propelling me out of the comfort of my bed. I threw on some clothes and headed for the backyard, pouring my frustration into productive effort. By day's end, the boys and I had completed the yard work and organized both the tool and the family storage sheds.

Meanwhile, Sandy's anger turned to tears. Soon after I abandoned our room, she crawled out of the covers. However, by the end of breakfast the CFS was taking its toll, sending her back to bed, retreating under the ever-protective covers.

SANDY

Tears quickly consumed me as I returned to the refuge of my bed, too fatigued from the stress to stay up. Exhausted from the lack of sleep and wounded by God's seeming lack of concern, I could no longer hold back the floodgates. "God, how can you be so uncaring?" I whimpered. "It's beginning to feel like you're never here for me in my desperation. We need you to step in and show us you care. Is that so much to ask?" The new wave of tears made it impossible to continue speaking, but my thoughts were still free to articulate the ache of my heart. *I don't understand. You didn't stop the torture when I was just a little girl, you won't take away this debilitating fatigue, and you aren't sending money to pay for the furniture! Do you simply not care? God, it seems that nothing we pray for gets answered lately!* Letting that last line settle in, I became resolute: *Oh, just forget it. We'll figure it out on our own.*

With that, I yanked the covers over my head, adding a defiant end to my distressed and wounded outburst. I soon fell into a fitful sleep.

A few hours later I awoke to the clatter of the lawn mower. I felt as though I hadn't even slept. My earlier outburst added another element to my heartache. I was upset with myself for being so upset with God. I felt guilty. Yet I couldn't deny my feelings. I felt fortunate that God loved me enough to allow for my humanity. But it still hurt nonetheless. Exasperated, I rolled over and closed my eyes once again.

Soon it was my nose that roused me from my slumber. The guys were making themselves lunch, and the enticing aroma called out to my hungry stomach. I was unable to eat much breakfast, due to my exhaustion, and now I could feel the effects of the lack of nourishment. I laid there, still too fatigued to function, and hoped my family would remember their bedridden mother and bring me something to eat. Why I entertained such indulgences, I don't know. My sons hadn't done anything like that before, why would they start now?

*Scott will remember me!* I reassured myself, fighting to keep the dream alive as I lay there floating in and out of consciousness. A while later, hunger pains drove me to roll over and look at the clock: 2:30. My empty dream heightened my self-pity. *As usual, no one even considered that I might get hungry too! God doesn't care, and now my family doesn't either. This is so unfair!*

With that, a new wave of tears soaked my pillow. Righteous indignation forestalled any attempt to call out and ask for what I needed. They should know I need lunch without me having to beg for it. So I lay there alone and miserable, listening to the growls and moans of my empty stomach.

At five o'clock Scott finally graced the bedroom doorway. "Honey, will you be making dinner?"

The fires of hell were no match for the wrath I poured out on my unsuspecting husband. "Are you kidding me?" I seethed. "Not only have I been in bed all day, but no one even stopped to consider that I might need lunch! Now that you all are hungry, you have the audacity to come in here and ask if I'm making dinner!"

I might have thrown my pillow if I'd had the strength. The fire of my fury was quickly shut off with the closing door; Scott had retreated in a hurry. With the aid of my anger, I pulled myself up in bed and in a huff, grabbed the latest book I'd been reading.

Within thirty minutes Scott was graciously setting dinner on my lap. It was his usual: scrambled eggs and toast. Though far from my favorite, it was much better than his sickly-sweet version of goulash, the only other meal in his limited repertoire. Besides, I was not going to look a gift horse in the mouth. I gratefully choked down the rubbery eggs and over-buttered toast, thanking him profusely for such kindness.

SCOTT

Having had the afternoon to blow off some steam and engage in a few thought-provoking conversations with God, I was ready to share my shift in attitude with Sandy. But when I'd presented her with what I quickly realized was a none-too-sensitive request for dinner, it became clear I'd blown my opportunity to share my epiphany. I figured the least I could do was to make her a nice, hot dinner as a peace offering. So I served up my specialty: scrambled eggs and toast. I cooked nearly two dozen eggs, enough to feed the five of us, so Sandy wouldn't have to get up. I lamented neglecting her lunch, but I'd assumed she'd taken care of that herself.

My anger had served me well, though. Not only did I get a lot accomplished around the house, but my outrage gave me the momentum I needed to wrench myself free from my inertia of helplessness. Throughout the afternoon, after a morning of silent ranting, I took a good, hard look at where our thoughts had previously taken a wrong turn. Now that Sandy had finished her dinner and seemed to be in better spirits, I decided to share my insights with her.

"I'm sorry for my insensitivity; I hope you're feeling better." I figured we'd get farther if I acknowledged her frustration. No matter how it felt to her, I really did care. "I wanted to share what I've been thinking today."

"It's okay. I know I let my self-pity get the best of me. Sorry for yelling at you like that. It has been a difficult day. So, what have you been thinking?"

"We really got off track."

"How so?" Sandy prompted.

"I believe that in our desperation, we deluded ourselves into believing that God *told* us to buy the furniture. As I was praying today, it hit me that God never told us to do that. I can't believe we thought such a thing. I've been kicking myself all afternoon for such a stupid decision!"

"You know, you're right," Sandy admitted. "Though I'm still frustrated, I agree. God didn't create this new mess. We did," she ended, with a sigh. "I was pretty upset with him earlier when I wasn't feeling well. Now I regret how I lashed out at him. He does care, even when it doesn't feel like it."

Caught up in my own thoughts, I continued. "God had nothing to do with our choice; we made that all on our own. Getting angry with him isn't going to change anything. Neither he, nor anyone else, twisted our arm and forced us to make this purchase. We acted on impulse, and we need to take responsibility. We are going to have to do our best to pay this bill on our own. We made the choice; we'll accept the consequences. It really has nothing to do with God's blessings." I paused just a moment to catch my breath as the fervor of my realization amped up my intensity.

Taking advantage of my momentary silence, Sandy jumped in. "I see your point. We aren't being punished or abandoned. We're just dealing with a natural law of cause and effect. We made a decision, and, just like any other decision, we need to live with it. It's just that this decision was wrapped around so many emotions it felt like it was all about God. The truth is God has been blessing our lives all along. Look at how well the guys are doing, in spite of all they've been through. Look at how much progress I've made since my breakdown, even though the doctors didn't give me much hope. When other families might have given up on each other, ours has actually grown closer. God's blessing is evident all over our lives. We became so fixated on our lack, that's all we saw."

"Yes, that's exactly my conclusion. God hears our prayers and he answers our prayers. Just because he doesn't always answer them the way we expect doesn't mean he's turned a deaf ear. This was just a good life lesson. Thankfully, he still loves and accepts us, even when we make blunders like this, I concluded.

# SURVIVAL SKILL

# *Take Personal Responsibility*

> Man must cease attributing his problems to his environment, and learn again to exercise his will—his personal responsibility.
>
> Albert Einstein

SCOTT AND SANDY

Up to this point, we had benefited greatly from our newly discovered *Survival Skills.* The art of *Acceptance* helped move us forward by accepting the reality of our situation. The skill of looking for the *Good* helped us find meaning and a sense of purpose in our suffering. Telling ourselves the *Truth* helped us eliminate stories that were complicating our troubles. These skills had truly helped us survive our life, and they were largely responsible for getting us as far as we had come. However, something was still missing. Deep inside, we both experienced a restless emptiness, an overwhelming sense of lack, a deficiency that rolled in on the heels of our many losses. The resulting furniture episode left us broken—financially and emotionally.

This rather embarrassing blunder (tuition in the school of life) was a decision we would not have normally made. Up to this point, our purchases had always been determined by one uncompromising principle: if we don't have the money, we don't buy it. Our unbending mantra yielded to necessity, however, when we were faced with Sandy's hospitalization and our family's medical and therapy costs. We were no longer on our way to financial independence. Our experiences had changed us. This staggering blow decimated our finances, demoralized our spirits, and ushered a greedy monster into our lives, a goblin known as *lack!*

The lack within grew restless. The absence it conjured was nearly palpable. It was as though a black hole had entered our lives, swallowing any contentment and hope, leaving us feeling vulnerable and deeply deprived. We were desperate for God's blessing to emerge in some tangible way. As this lack further invaded our lives, we became needy, looking for anything or anyone to help us. A sense of entitlement pervaded our thoughts and feelings: *We deserve a break. Haven't we been through enough?* We longed for God to take up our cause and rescue us from this all-encompassing need. We expected him to restore what we perceived had been unjustly taken.

This expectation wasn't just about tangible things or even money. Attaining stuff really wasn't that important to us. Our desire for physical replacement was simply an outward reflection of an inner emotional ache. We were still recovering from all that had happened; our hearts were as depleted as our bank accounts. We longed to experience God's love as concrete and visible. We had mistakenly equated the replacement of our losses and Sandy's physical healing with a demonstration of his love. This would be proof, we reasoned, that God was aware of our suffering and sacrifices and was pleased with our obedience, providing physical evidence that he cared.

This debilitating need and unquenchable longing created false expectations and left no room for God's plan, will, or sovereignty.

We had adopted the belief that if we had enough faith, God would answer our prayers according to our own desires. After all, he can do anything, so how could he deny such impassioned, hope-filled requests? As we came across testimonies of others who had been miraculously healed and restored, our belief that God would do the same for us increased. However, when it became clear that God was not going to act according to our expectations, we were devastated. Yet we later realized that God used this experience as a catalyst to move us into a new, more purposeful direction and ultimately, out of the clutches of lack.

We also discovered something significant about our prayers. We realized that our faith that God would grant our request was driven more by faith in our faith than faith in God. Faith in our faith says, "Once we have enough faith, then God will grant our request." Faith in God says, "We pray, believing for what we ask, while allowing for and deferring to his divine plan for our life."

Contrary to some beliefs, God is not a magical genie existing only to grant our every wish. He is our all-knowing and all-loving Father, who acts in our best and highest interest always, even when it conflicts with our own desires and even when it makes us angry and upset.

It was during this time of discouragement and confusion that we discovered our fourth Survival Skill: *Assuming Personal Responsibility.*

We realized that if we were to change or improve our situation, we needed to proceed responsibly. This meant we needed to stop blaming God for our condition and be accountable for this place in which we found ourselves. This did not mean we were to blame for the pain, trauma, and loss that had pierced our lives against our will, but we *were* responsible for our reactions, responses, and choices. We also needed to stop making excuses and quit looking for some miraculous bailout. In short, we needed to assume responsibility to do whatever we could to move forward.

In a nutshell, taking personal responsibility means assuming ownership for my thoughts, words, choices, decisions, actions, and reactions.

Personal responsibility is assuming ownership of my thoughts, words, choices, decisions, actions, and reactions.

## Our Life, God's Power

There is a harmonious balance between our responsibility and God's direction and empowerment. His role is obviously foundational to ours. We find this exemplified in the book of Ephesians 6:10: "God is strong, and he wants you strong. So take everything the Master has set out for you, well-made weapons of the best materials. And put them to use so you will be able to stand up to everything the Devil throws your way" (MSG). God equips us with everything we need; therefore, he expects us to do our part. Notice the action words used: *take, put them to use,* and *stand.* These actions are ours to take, and they represent our part of the equation. In other words, it is our responsibility to actively plug into God's supernatural, life-changing power and walk it out in our daily lives. When we practice personal responsibility, through God's strength, we enter into a partnership with God that is essential to change and improve our situation.

## What Are We Responsible For?

Below we have included practical areas that each of us is personally responsible for.

I am responsible for:

- My choices: My choices and decisions are mine, and mine alone, to own.
- Getting my needs met: I can't expect others to read my mind and know what my needs are. Nor can I expect others to be responsible for meeting my needs.
- My behaviors: I am responsible for my behaviors and actions.
- My reactions: My reactions are always about me and are within my realm of control.
- Where my life is today: Though I may not be responsible for bad things that have happened to me against my will, I am responsible for my reactions and any choices that have contributed to my current condition.
- Moving forward: I am responsible for doing whatever is necessary in order to move forward.
- My emotions and thoughts: I take ownership of my thoughts and emotions and do what I need to do to bring them in line with Christ and keep them on a healthy track.
- My words: I am responsible for what I say and how I say it.
- My self-care: It is up to me to take care of the body, mind, and spirit that God entrusted to my care.

---

## IT'S YOUR TURN

Have you assumed full responsibility for doing everything within your power, through God's strength, to improve or change your painful circumstances? Fill out the following assessment to see how well you have been doing.

Have I Failed to Take Personal Responsibility?

- ☐ I've been blaming my circumstances, others, and even God for my suffering.
- ☐ I've been making excuses for not doing what I need to do to improve my situation.
- ☐ I've been using my painful experiences as an excuse for my irresponsible choices.
- ☐ I've been justifying my negative actions and reactions.
- ☐ Though I've prayed things would improve, I haven't done everything I could do to better my situation.
- ☐ I haven't "stepped up to the plate" when I've needed to.
- ☐ I've felt powerless in my circumstances and relationships.
- ☐ I've been relying on others to take care of me and rescue me from my struggles.
- ☐ I've been angry at God for not changing me or my circumstances.

How did you do? Don't worry if you checked off more than you would have liked. This is no indication of your value as a person, but it does help explain why you may have felt victimized. Without realizing or intending it, every time you blamed others, made excuses, became overly dependent on others, or developed unrealistic expectations of God, you inadvertently gave up your personal responsibility. In so doing, you have relinquished your God-given empowerment necessary to change your circumstances.

## Steps to Taking Personal Responsibility

The following steps can help you reclaim your God-given personal responsibility. By doing so, you can move through your pain in a cooperative effort with him.

### *Own Up*

There are two aspects to this survival skill of personal responsibility. The first is to accept where your life is at this moment and take responsibility for any role you played in getting to this place. The second is to take every reasonable and responsible step needed to move forward from here. You will never be able to effectively move forward until you first assume ownership for your life as it is.

Though you may not be responsible for the terrible things that happened against your will and beyond your ability to control, you can assume ownership for your life as it is now. You can't always control what happens to you, but you are responsible for how you respond to, and the choices you make regarding, your painful experiences.

The second aspect consists of taking responsibility for doing whatever it takes (thoughts, choices, decisions, and actions) to forge ahead and change or improve your circumstances. Many struggle to get to this point. They find themselves trapped in their pain, unable to move forward. Rather than accessing their God-empowered ability that comes in assuming personal responsibility, they relinquish it by blaming others, making excuses, overly depending on others, and falling into a victim mentality.

> Make no mistake: God does not *need* our action, nor are we to *work* our way into his good graces. This has nothing to do with our salvation, which is his free gift to all. God loves us even when we choose to remain in our beds, so to speak, with

> the covers pulled over our heads, refusing to engage in life. His love and acceptance are ultimate and completely unconditional. Our working out our personal responsibility is for our own benefit.

## *Stop Blaming*

We will be the first to admit that it is easy to blame circumstances, others, and even God for our pain and misfortunes. Soon after Sandy's hospitalization, we blamed both Cat and, at times, God for our suffering. Some might argue that we had a perfectly good reason to blame Cat. However, blaming did absolutely nothing to improve our situation. Staying in the blaming mode actually made things worse and moved us farther away from the possibility of change.

No matter how justifiable your blame-shifting may appear, every time you succumb to the blame game you are literally handing control of your happiness, well-being, and freedom to someone or something else. To make matters worse, this is often the person or problem to whom you least want to hand over control. More importantly, you give away your God-empowered ability to change or improve your situation. As a result, you will feel victimized and powerless.

Take your focus off others and shine it on yourself. Take responsibility for your role in your life as it currently is. You'll find it very empowering.

> Blaming circumstances and others for your suffering merely hands over your God-empowered ability to change or improve your circumstances to whatever and whomever you are blaming.

## *No More Excuses*

Excuses come so easily, don't they? "But you don't understand what I've been through!" "It's not my fault!" "You just don't know what this feels like!" "I'm waiting on God to change things." "I'm waiting on so and so to change first." "Things will never change anyway, so why try?"

Like blame, excuses keep you from taking personal responsibility. These toxic paralyzers breed inactivity and passivity, numbing you from your God-given potential. Making excuses is simply a way of justifying why you do what you ought not, and why you don't do what you ought.

Gaining freedom from your prison of suffering requires work on your part. It won't just magically happen. You can't afford yourself the luxury of making excuses. If you are not careful, you will excuse your way into permanent victimization. There may be many reasons why you haven't done what you've needed to do up to this point. However, if you are to move past your pain, you will need to declare: "No more excuses!"

Bill Purvis, pastor of Cascades Hills Church in Columbus, Georgia, says, "In most areas, people do what they really want to do. They either make a *way* or make an *excuse*."

How about you? Is your energy going into making a way for change or making excuses to stay the same?

## *Let Go of the Desire to Be Rescued*

When we are down and out, broken, powerless, helpless, hopeless, or desperate, it is easy to fall into the trap of wanting to be rescued. You might wish Indiana Jones would save you from your proverbial pit of deadly vipers (of course, he hates snakes too). Perhaps Zorro or Robin Hood could take up your cause, liberating you from all that is corrupt and unjust. More realistically, though, it might be a spouse, a family member, or a friend on whom you are overly dependent. Maybe you've placed your doctor on an unrealistic pedestal, expecting him or her to put an end to your suffering. Possibly you depend on the advice and direction of a pastor as if he were God himself, leaving no room for the human factor.

Let's face it: all of us, at one time or another, have experienced some idealistic expectation of rescue.

SANDY

I must admit, there have been times while struggling with chronic fatigue syndrome when I have found my mind entertaining rescue scenarios, usually while sitting in a practitioner's office. CFS is not widely understood and as a result, in the early years was not always taken seriously by my doctors. "You're just depressed" was often the professional diagnosis. "It's just in your head" was what I heard. My longing for release from the taxing exhaustion, as well as the lack of understanding and compassion I frequently received, was overwhelming. It even progressed to the point that I concluded I might be taken more seriously if I were to faint while in the waiting area. Of course, I would die of embarrassment if I did and would never intentionally try. Yet that didn't stop my mind from rehearsing such an attention-getting ploy.

More commonly, however, the focus of my rescue desires was aimed at Scott. When the CFS knocked me flat on my back for weeks on end, it would create another hardship for the family, especially Scott. With all we'd been through, he was worn out and his expressions of compassion lacked the luster they once carried. In moments of despair and loneliness, I would find myself longing for Scott's attentiveness, believing that somehow his care and devotion were the missing keys to get me on my feet again.

However, I discovered that when he went the extra mile, even when he catered to my every whim, such devoted accommodation did not provide me what I hoped it would. I eventually realized I was making Scott accountable for my well-being. This tragic error did neither of us any good. Something had to change! I began by taking responsibility for my feelings. Through further introspection, I investigated the debilitating emotions my illness elicited. Once I narrowed them down, I sought help in working through them. By taking charge of my own well-being, I allowed Scott to resume the rightful position as my husband and not my savior. The balance in our marriage was once again restored.

SCOTT AND SANDY

Can you identify any areas in your life where you have longed for some idealistic rescue? It is extremely destructive to defer your own personal responsibility to others. When this happens, not only do you relinquish your God-given ability to change or improve your circumstances, but you eventually develop unrealistic expectations of those on whom you are relying. As a result, you expect more from them than they are equipped to provide. Consequently, they will fail and let you down. This then perpetuates your cycle of disappointment and hopelessness.

When you begin to see this need for what it is, an area in your life that needs your attention, you are free to take responsibility to restore health to that area.

Assuming personal responsibility does not preclude you from enlisting the help and support of others. There is a major difference between reliance (dependence) and enlisting the support (interdependence or mutual dependence) of others. You were not created to be an island or to travel this journey alone. Asking for help when it is needed is both healthy and responsible. Sometimes taking personal responsibility means asking for help.

Perhaps God is waiting expectantly for you to get fed up with your situation and finally take action. Regardless of your pain or hardship, we encourage you to step into your God-given power and stop looking to others for what God knows you can do for yourself.

No one can do for you what you need to do for yourself.

## *Eliminate Any Victim Mindset*

Closely related to the need to be rescued is a victim mindset, both of which remove personal responsibility. What is a victim mindset? In its basic form, a victim mindset is a state of mind produced by feelings of helplessness where the control and responsibility for one's life is left in the hands of others. A victim mentality is a thought process that is characterized by any or all of the following:

## *Characteristics of a Victim Mentality*

- Fatalistic thinking: I never get a break. Bad things always happen to me. My life will always be difficult.
- Helpless thinking: I am unable to help myself.
- Self-pity: My situation is worse that anyone's.
- Sympathy seeking: I need others to feel sorry for me and understand how difficult my struggles are.
- Dependency: I need someone to do this for me.
- Martyr: I proudly display my problems to elicit admiration and sympathy for my sacrifices and suffering.
- Doormat: I can't say no.
- Blame: My problems are someone else's fault.

- Reactivity: I hold others responsible for my anger and defensive reactions.
- Resentment: I hold on to the wrongs committed against me.
- Entitlement: The world owes me. God owes me.
- Chaotic: My circumstances control me and my emotional well-being.

The real danger of victim thinking is that it results in victim living. Think as a victim and you will live as a victim. A victim mentality is the antithesis of personal responsibility. If you have taken on a victim mindset, challenge these thoughts with the corresponding list of true and responsible beliefs we have provided below.

## *Countering a Victim Mentality*

- Fatalistic thinking > Forward thinking: Things might not be great for me now, but a change in my attitude can make this easier. There's always something to be hopeful for.
- Helpless thinking > Competent thinking: Through Christ, I can do whatever it takes to get through this. (Philippians 4:13)
- Self-pity > Sympathetic toward others: There is always someone who has it worse than I do. I can make it.
- Sympathy seeking > Courageous thinking: I can step out and do what I need to do without the sympathy of others.
- Dependency > Empowered: God has given, and will continue to provide, all I need to deal with my situation.

- Martyr > Competent: I do not need the acknowledgment and attention from others to do what is required.
- Doormat > Assertive: I say no when I need to, without having to justify it.
- Blame > Personal responsibility: I do not need to assign fault, I take responsibility for my own actions and reactions.
- Reactivity > Accountability: My reactions are always about me and I hold myself accountable for them.
- Resentment > Forgiveness: I give all retribution over to God, and I release others from the prison of my bitterness. In so doing, I release myself as well.
- Entitlement > Contribution: What can I give back?
- Chaotic > Management: Through the empowerment of my personal responsibility, I take ownership of my life and choose how I respond to each and every circumstance. I take responsibility for doing whatever I need in order to move my life wherever it needs to be.

Letting go of your victim mindset will require courage, dedication, and hard work on your part. But we believe that you will be glad you did. As with every area of your life, the choice is yours.

## *Take Action*

Personal responsibility is decision based and action oriented. It is proactive rather than passive or reactive.

What is one proactive step you could take right now that would immediately change, or at least improve, your situation? What has God been prompting you to do? What have others been encouraging you to do? Adopt the Nike slogan and just do it! Maybe reading this book is the first step for you. Taking care of yourself and making sure that you get enough rest, proper diet, and exercise is also a good starting point.

Victim thinking results in victim living.

## *Let Go of All False Responsibility*

Whereas some tend to avoid assuming responsibility, others go to the opposite extreme and become overly responsible, taking on the responsibility that rightly belongs to others. We refer to this as false responsibility. This is a common affliction for type-A personalities, people pleasers, nurturers, and natural leaders.

Remember, personal responsibility is just that: personal. It is yours and yours alone. No one can do for you what you need to do for yourself. Correspondingly, you cannot do for others what they must do for themselves. As we stated earlier, God never intended for us to shoulder what is not ours to carry. He has given each person the grace needed to walk in their personal responsibility. God gives us the grace to support one another but not to take over the responsibility that rightly belongs to others.

This tendency to take on false responsibility and over-function on behalf of others was a major contributing factor in Sandy's breakdown, which we shared earlier in this book. Sandy had been taking care of everyone except herself. Believe us, the consequences are simply not worth the price. Besides feeling unappreciated and taken advantage of, those who over-function on behalf of others often set themselves up to be the bad guy and scapegoat when things don't work out.

If you are going to support others, make certain your focus is to help them help themselves. Pray for wisdom before helping. Check your motives. If they are self-serving in nature (makes me feel better about myself, avoids conflict, eliminates guilt, creates dependency, and provides me with a sense of control) ask God to help you resist your compulsion to take on this false responsibility. Otherwise, you're not really helping the other person. Actually, you're damaging them and yourself.

Over-functioning enables others and
sets you up to be the bad guy.

## CONCLUSION

The intent of this chapter has not been to make you feel in any way irresponsible. Rather, our goal is to help you positively change your circumstances by taking on your personal responsibility and stepping into your God-given empowerment.

Though you may be passive by nature, dig deep, pray for strength, and take action. Though assuming responsibility for others in your life may be second nature to you, stop! Though you may have good reasons to blame, choose not to. Though there may be a plethora of excuses, determine not to use them. Though a part of you may long to be rescued, let that go. Instead, engage your strong self that's been tucked away in the shadows and step up to the plate on your own behalf.

We encourage you to take responsibility for your life, not because you should but because you can. It will make all the difference in the world. We believe in you. Believe in yourself and in the Lord. Partner with him, as he's working for your good. Together you can do it.

# *Finding Freedom*

SANDY

The calendar had just turned, ushering in a new decade. We'd all survived the ultimately innocuous, globally anticipated perils of Y2K and life had settled into a calm rhythm. The furniture bill was gradually becoming easier to pay, though it kept us fairly strapped. My therapeutic work with Samantha was coming to a close, and I was in a mentally and emotionally strong, sound place.

Scott had taken on a new project, the restoration of an older model Chevy Caprice. He wasn't necessarily looking for a project to take on, but the car we had was quite cramped and this old Chevy he stumbled upon would give us the additional space we needed. He calculated that with the parts being relatively inexpensive, he could create a "new" car for the family at a fraction of the cost. It was a bargain he couldn't pass up. Ironically, six months later, Scott found an older Chevy Suburban that gave us all the room we needed, but he continued to refurbish this car, as by now, it was his obsession.

Many evenings and weekends were devoted to the renovation, our sons often joining in on this male-bonding project. Eventually, Scott's hard work paid off and this older vehicle was transformed to its former splendor. With his venture nearly complete, Scott spent hours doting over his metallic baby, waxing and polishing, vacuuming and dusting, poking and prodding.

This beautiful, seventy-degree Saturday late in November, was no different for Scott than most had been lately. Having already double-checked the fluids, which he'd triple-checked the week before and the week before that, he knelt beside his beloved masterpiece, inspecting the air-pressure of each tire.

Meanwhile, our youngest son and I had begun our yearly ritual of putting up our Christmas lights. Years prior, he was the only one whose arm I could twist into helping me with this two-person task. We had such fun that year that he decided to make the light hanging his permanent job. This year I had given him free rein to display his artistic skills on the roof. He took to the height like a mountain goat and to his shingled canvas like Picasso.

Our house sat on the corner of a quiet, sleepy little side street and a busy, raucous road that separated us from the elementary school yard. While our son carefully worked his creative magic up high, I worked safely on the ground, draping lights around our picket fence. The fence separated the section of the front yard that was landscaped in gravel and river rock from the back half, which sported a green carpet of grass. In spite of the obnoxious traffic, I felt comfortable that my family was protected within the embrace of the sturdy and now festively lit barrier.

## SCOTT

I looked up from my spot beside the rear tire and saw that the Christmas decorations were shaping up nicely. I knew our youngest, being quite creative, was excited to have been handed the reins this year. I was anxious for nightfall, when we could illuminate his brilliant handiwork.

In spite of everything going on around me, I refocused on my prized possession: the 1977 Chevy Caprice Landau. With the help of a mechanic friend and a few automotive how-to manuals I enjoyed dedicating my free time to restoring this car to its original condition. Finally, after many hours of hard work and sacrifice, I was driving our "new" car. It was mechanically sound and easy on the eyes. I had buffed out the exterior paint, removing the oxidation. I could almost see my own reflection. The old, cracked vinyl roof had been replaced, and the interior was now restored, emitting that new-car smell. To say that I was proud of this labor of love was a huge understatement. After examining the last tire, I slowly stood from my kneeling position and took a moment to admire my treasure.

This week I planned to take her in to be appraised in order to obtain comprehensive insurance to cover the increased value. Up to this point I had only carried limited liability coverage, but in my own driveway what did I have to worry about?

Discovering a smudge, I tugged my tee-shirt out of my waistband and rubbed the soft fabric across the rear fender, removing the offending smear. As I massaged the glossy surface, I thanked God, recounting the long hours and many sacrifices that had gone into making this dream a reality. Caught up in my reverie, I barely heard the revving engine, but Sandy's hair-raising scream certainly grabbed my attention.

SANDY

I had just climbed the ladder and had both arms full of lights and extension cords when I heard the sound of an engine roaring in the distance. Reckless speeding down our street was quite commonplace, extremely annoying, and very dangerous.

"The speed limit is only thirty miles per hour, for goodness' sakes!" I shouted to no one in particular, since the driver certainly couldn't hear me. Tempted to turn around and send the lawbreaker a dirty look, I resisted and reached up to hand a string of lights to our son.

Before I could pass off the bundle, I nearly fell off the ladder. A deafening *pop* rang through the air, as if someone had fired a gun. Regaining my balance, I turned just in time to see a huge, rusty bucket of a van bouncing off our neighbor's curb and heading for our house. The driver was off course and coming fast—way too fast. My stomach lurched. In that split second I realized the stray vehicle was barreling straight toward my unsuspecting husband. Scott was facing his beloved car, his back to the van, completely unaware of his impending doom.

The warning left my mouth before I could form it into words. Its force started in my toes and resonated throughout my entire being. My only chance to save my husband, this scream, would mean the difference between life and death.

As my terrified voice rang out, the rampaging van hit our corner of the intersection and within milliseconds had zipped up our river-rock retaining wall. The speeding hunk of metal was sent skyward by the rocky embankment. It flew with startling grace over the fire hydrant and with lightning speed, traveled straight for Scott.

*Oh God, my husband is going to die,* was the last thought that registered before I heard the terrible, bone-jarring crash.

## SCOTT

Alerted by Sandy's shocking, high-pitched alarm, I turned and looked behind me, not at Sandy, but in the direction of a strange noise that caught my attention. This heaven-directed decision saved my life. Had I looked at Sandy first, I would have lost valuable seconds of my limited response time. As I turned, my eyes were met with a staggering image that my mind struggled to comprehend. The sight of it paralyzed me. I was in the flight path of a 1969 Dodge missile. The arrow-straight ease with which it flew belied its great size and weight.

Everything suddenly began to move in slow motion as my mind fought to comprehend the danger. It was as if time had stopped. I had read about this phenomenon but had never experienced it until now. Waking to my predicament, I tried to move but couldn't. My feet were one with the concrete. It was as if I was bound and held in place by some unseen force.

With a jolt, time resumed its normal pace, and at the last possible second my legs began to move. I covered the ten feet of driveway with lightning speed, hitting the garage door running, narrowly escaping certain death.

The screeching and grinding of metal sent shockwaves through my body as I made my narrow escape. It was all so surreal. Out of harm's way, my overloaded senses took a moment to sort through what had just happened.

The heavy van had crashed into my newly restored car, its point of impact precisely where I'd stood only a split second before. My prized car was crushed between the offending van and our three-quarter ton Chevy Suburban, which was parked next to her in our driveway. The force of the collision was so great that it literally shoved my Caprice and our Suburban six feet into our neighbor's driveway, narrowly missing their car. *Wow! My body would have been unrecognizable sandwiched in this mangled mess of twisted metal!*

Stunned at the scene before me, not even Sandy's horrified voice broke through my stupor as she rushed to my side. "Scott, honey, are you okay? Are you hurt?" I could feel her arms around me as she clung to me. I could hear her voice, but nothing registered in my state of shock.

Finally, the revving engine and the noxious mix of boiling antifreeze, leaking gasoline, and old, hot motor oil grabbed my attention, propelling me into action. Assuring Sandy I was okay, I ran to check on the van's occupants.

Meanwhile, the clash of ripping metal sent our two older sons running out from our house and our youngest scrambling down from the roof. They couldn't believe their eyes. Sandy had the presence of mind to call for help and borrowed one of our sons' ever-present cell phones to dial emergency services.

"Take your foot off the gas," I yelled through the closed window at the surprisingly uninjured driver. I opened the door and saw no other passengers and no outward signs of trauma on the driver, other than the fact that he was completely disoriented.

I shouted again, over the roar of the engine, "Take your foot off the gas!" The bewildered man just stared back at me.

After a moment he finally recovered enough to respond, "My foot isn't on the pedal. The accelerator must be stuck."

"Turn off the ignition," I yelled. He fumbled with the keys, and soon the engine quieted, leaving an eerie silence in its wake.

The driver stumbled out of the wreckage, his eyes crazed with fear. "Are you okay?" I asked, as he began shaking his arms and hands and took up a nervous pacing in a tight circle. His movements were erratic and frenzied.

"I-I ... I gotta ... I gotta walk. I gotta walk," he insisted. His mumbling was frantic and disjointed as he hurried away.

Assuming he just needed some space to calm down, I turned my attention to the flammables leaking from the wreck. Worried about the possibility of an explosion, I quickly gathered any containers I could find to catch the oozing fluids. With the help of my sons, we kept the gathering crowd away from the chaos, making sure no one was smoking.

I didn't have time to agonize over what had just happened—the loss of my car and my own near-death experience. The danger was not yet over; there would be time for thinking and feeling later.

Within moments two fire engines arrived to contain the explosive fluids. I breathed a sigh of relief as the professionals sprayed the protective foam over the danger zone. The collision was bad enough; an explosion would have been disastrous.

As the firemen contained their end of the situation, two patrol cars pulled up. The police officers examined the scene and asked for our statements. They quickly noticed the absence of the driver and asked his whereabouts. Sandy explained that he had said he needed to walk and she'd assumed he'd be right back.

The officer went to his car and called for a helicopter to track the driver down. Sandy, still holding our son's cell phone, called her friend Linda, who lived around the corner and down the block, to tell her of all the excitement. As they talked, Linda asked Sandy to describe the driver. Linda couldn't believe it. She had been working in the yard just moments before when a man matching the description had asked her for money and directions to get out of the neighborhood. Thanking Linda for the tip, Sandy hung up and ran to the first officer, giving him her friend's address. He took off in his cruiser while he informed the helicopter circling overhead.

In the meantime, the boys and I followed the second officer as he retraced the trajectory the van followed. The officer estimated the van to be traveling at least fifty-five miles an hour. The loud *pop* we had heard must have been his right tire blowing out as it hit our neighbor's curb. When this happened, it caused the vehicle to veer off its present course and angle itself toward our property. The van then hit our rock retaining wall at precisely the perfect speed and angle to launch it into the air.

As we left the street and walked onto our yard, we were amazed that this large beast of a vehicle cleared the small space between the city streetlight on the corner and our little fence. It just barely fit between the two, with no room for error. Upon closer observation, we could see a scrape of white paint on the inside of the light post and a more significant one along the slats of our red fence. In its flight, it also managed to clear the fire hydrant in our front yard.

The officer concluded, "Wow, you should have been killed! A higher power was definitely watching over you today!" I barely had time to consider his inference when the first officer pulled up in the patrol car, toting a wild-eyed passenger. The officer helped the handcuffed man out of the backseat and asked us to identify him. The man hung his head in shame as he was positively identified by each of us.

After placing him back into the car, the first officer returned to us and explained that the driver was definitely under the influence of some sort of drug and would be going to jail. He went on to explain that the van belonged to the girlfriend of the driver. As if losing both our vehicles and nearly my life weren't enough, the officer informed us that the driver of the van had no insurance coverage. "Who's going to pay for this mess and replace my car?" I agonized loudly, to no one in particular. Having no reassuring answers, the officers soon left.

With the officers gone and the firemen having left earlier, the show was over. The crowd began to disperse, while a couple of helpful neighbors remained to join in the cleanup.

I took advantage of a few reflective moments and circled the scene, unable to stand still. As I replayed the event in my mind, I struggled to comprehend all that had just happened. I moved to survey the situation from the vantage point of where I had been standing when it all went down. I was again amazed at how precisely everything occurred. *Wow, this would have been the perfect way to take me out!* Had any one thing happened differently, the course of this airborne demon of destruction would have been altered. Circumstances were perfect for my demise with one exception: Sandy's warning. It saved my life.

The officer's words about a higher being watching over me reached me at a deeper level. I suddenly felt comforted at the thought that God had intervened and saved my life. I was overwhelmed by his love and protection. *Thank you God, this was truly a miracle!*

No sooner had my gratitude been offered when another thought sent a shiver down my spine: *Was it possible that another powerful being had tried to orchestrate my demise?* It suddenly felt as though I had a giant bull's eye on my back, making me feel extremely vulnerable.

Over the next few weeks, I was thankful that I wasn't dead. However, I was enraged at the driver; his lack of judgment and dangerous lifestyle nearly cost me my life and had completely destroyed my car.

During this time I also began to suffer from the post traumatic stress symptoms that often occur after surviving a traumatic experience. I started experiencing panic attacks and developed a hypersensitive startle response.

Sandy and I now faced yet an additional stressor: the need to purchase another vehicle. The Suburban needed repair and the "new" car was totaled. With no insurance coverage to pull from the driver of the van and only liability coverage on my restoration project, we had to come up with money to purchase another vehicle—money we didn't have. We went to our bank and took out a line of credit, which allowed us to purchase a 1989 Caprice Classic. We were further able to consolidate our debts and pay off our furniture loan.

• • •

SANDY

"Hi, Sandy, I have something for you," Samantha excitedly greeted me at what was one of our final sessions together. "You've mentioned several times how you'd love to work with women who are going through difficult times. Well, I might have found a perfect opportunity for you." With that, Sam handed me a newspaper clipping. "I also went online and checked this out. From all I've read, I think this is right up your alley."

"Life coach?" I pondered, scanning the first few lines of the article. "I've never heard of such a thing."

"Take this home and do some investigating. Personally, after spending the last year or so working with you, I believe you'd make a great life coach. Study up on it, pray about it, and let me know what you think."

I was honored that Sam had researched this on my behalf and had such confidence in me. I did feel I had much to offer wounded women, especially on the heels of my own journey, but I didn't realize Sam felt this strongly about it.

The next several days were spent reading all I could about life coaching. It was a relatively new field, so there wasn't an overabundance of information, but I really connected with the concept. Although most coaches at that time focused on the corporate arena, I discovered that many had begun working with private individuals, helping them improve their lives.

I was initially concerned because of my incomplete college education. Even with a heart for women and much personal experience, I was in no way qualified as a counselor. It was a relief to discover that as a coach I would never be diagnosing, psychoanalyzing, or providing psychotherapy. A coach does not work with mental illness.

I found it intriguing that coaching is a partnership between the client and coach. The articles I read explained that through powerful questions, a coach opens new possibilities to the client by providing a different perspective for their problem. Realizing their current condition and choosing to be present and future-focused, the client makes a decision about where they want to be in life. Accountability and goal setting are a large part of the process.

I shared all the information I'd gathered with Scott, and we both came to the same excited conclusion: I was suited for this kind of work. Soon I was adding coaching schools to my research. After much prayer and deliberation, I settled on Coach University. I was impressed with their comprehensive two-year curriculum and their recognized leadership in the coaching community. I couldn't believe I was actually on my way to fulfilling my heart's desire to help other women. I was grateful for Sam's belief in me.

Within weeks, I was settling into tele-classes at Coach U. The convenience of taking classes while at home worked well within my physical limitations of fatigue. Though nervous at first, I really enjoyed all I was learning. Scott was impressed to hear the practical approach the courses took. While in one class, I met a fellow student, Margaret, who was a year ahead of me in the program. I was surprised at the wisdom she showed while in class, so much so that I contacted her that day and hired her as my coach. As it would later turn out, Scott was also to glean much from Margaret's coaching skills.

SCOTT

"You just don't get it, Margaret. I have to work these long hours. I can't think of myself; my family is relying on me. Self-care is just impossible!"

"Scott, what you actually mean is that you are choosing to work those long hours and you are choosing not to do what you need to do in order to take care of yourself," Margaret countered. "What if you made a different choice?"

I can still remember this frustrating exchange between Margaret and me—frustrating, that is, on my part. I felt offended and even a little angry. The audacity of this woman, suggesting that I was choosing to live this way! I didn't choose this. If I actually could choose something, it certainly wouldn't be my life as it had been over the last ten years. I didn't enjoy all the responsibilities I carried for my family, nor did I relish the long hours spent helping my clients solve their problems so I could make ends meet. I had more than my fair share of problems to deal with. Frankly, I felt "problemed out."

Margaret simply didn't understand what I'd been through, I reasoned. No one could. She seemed completely unmoved by all the sacrifices I'd made and the inner pain that I still carried, even though I thought I'd articulated them quite clearly during our session.

*What does she know, anyway? She's a single woman who's never had to shoulder the responsibility of providing for a family. I'm glad this coaching is working for Sandy, but I'm not so sure it is for me.*

This was my first meeting with Margaret, and though I was trying to be polite, I was upset. It was Sandy who had actually set up the appointment, saying it was my turn to receive some much-needed help. She was worried about me, and truth be told, I was a little worried about me too.

As our session came to a close, Margaret challenged me to consider the possibility that I had other choices. She encouraged me to step back from my situation in order to gain a different perspective before making a judgment. I thanked her and hung up the phone.

Conflicted, I stayed in my office and mentally replayed our conversation. Deep inside, I knew Margaret had nailed the problem: I was overworked and overly driven. Her answer to that problem, though very appealing, didn't seem doable. Sure, I could choose to not work so hard, but where would that get us? I just couldn't see any other choice.

Getting up, I opened the door and stepped into the kitchen, where Sandy waited with an expectant smile. That smile faded quickly, however, when she got a look at my face.

"What happened? It didn't go well?"

"Margaret was nice enough; I just don't think she understands our situation. She pushed the idea that I choose to work hard and that I am choosing to not take care of myself. Maybe she's right, but I just don't see any other way."

My frustration visible, Sandy walked over and put her arms around me. "Scott, you've sacrificed and labored for the boys and me for too long. I love you and appreciate all you've given up and done for us. You are a great provider. You've hung in there when many men would have walked away. Honestly, honey, beyond all God has done, it was your loving commitment that held us together all these years." Then she took a step back, gripped both my arms, and looked me square in the eye. "Scott, I love you, but Margaret's got a point. You do need to start taking care of yourself. You cannot continue to live like this. You don't need to shoulder everything any longer. I am not the helpless, messed-up woman I was. I'm your partner. And I've been trying to resume my place in our partnership, but you insist on continuing to do it all on your own. Let me share some of the load. Let me back in." She reached up and hugged me, choking out her final plea: "Please."

Later that day, I was back in my office cleaning my aquarium when Margaret's words came back to me: "What if you made a different choice?" Perhaps she was right. I'd never even considered another alternative. At that moment Sandy's plea rang through my spirit. "I am your partner … let me share the load … please."

As the water from the aquarium drained into my five-gallon bucket, I wondered: *Am I making a choice not to take care of myself? Maybe I* am *choosing to take on more than I need to carry. Maybe Sandy is right. Maybe I* do *need to make some different choices. Note to self: Set up another appointment with Margaret to discuss this further.*

• • •

SANDY

Five years had passed since Scott was confronted with his "choice-less thinking" and we'd reestablished our partnership, allowing me to share the load. I was seeing clients on a part-time basis, and we were conducting groups in local churches based on the survival skills.

Curled up on the couch, I chided myself as Scott headed out the door to lead that night's group alone. "I can't let Scott down again," I scolded. "I should be going with him tonight." A few months prior, the chronic fatigue had taken on the added component of pain and was re-diagnosed as fibromyalgia. The pain and fatigue made it increasingly difficult for me to co-lead these classes.

Just a few weeks before, we had taught the class on "Living in Choice," yet here I was, feeling stuck and choice-less. Although Scott never complained and was more than capable of leading the class alone, I was frustrated that I couldn't be there for him. It didn't seem fair for him to have to carry the load alone, although I was physically powerless to do anything about it. A wave of *déjà vu* swept over me, its undertow pulling me back to a time when Scott shouldered my responsibilities while I sat by helplessly.

As I struggled to keep my sinking emotions afloat, I recalled several conversations I'd had with Margaret years earlier. I often drew from the storehouse of wisdom I'd received from our weekly talks. One conversation in particular stood out this night, an exchange Margaret and I had about handling others' feelings. This conversation was the beginning of my deeper understanding of the power of choice.

> "Sandy, I understand you don't want to hurt your friend's feelings, but notice how your over-protectiveness of her is affecting you. What you are doing here is making a choice. You are

choosing to continue to put yourself last, which is why you are feeling angry right now. You always have a choice, and right now, you are choosing not to take care of yourself by refusing to set a boundary with your friend."

When Margaret presented me with the notion that I always had a choice, it didn't completely register at first, at least to the degree I needed. *Of course we have choices,* I thought. *Everybody knows that.* I was listening to Margaret but only hearing on a superficial level. At the time, I wasn't prepared to fully look at my life through the lens of choice.

Unwilling to allow me to settle for a shallow understanding, Margaret faithfully continued to approach the subject of choice week after week in our sessions together. With gentle reminders, she would keep the idea before me, compelling me to confront my limited thinking. She challenged me to go deeper, far below the surface, where lasting changes would be birthed and eventually take root, setting up permanent residence.

Seeing myself as always having choices was a difficult transition for me. I was indeed making choices, yet the opposite seemed so true. I genuinely felt as though others held more power or sway over my decisions than I did. I discovered that it had been easier for me to acquiesce, yielding to what I believed others wanted.

The people-pleasing side of me decided that as long as others dictated my life, I wasn't responsible or wrong if things didn't work out. Therefore, I was safe and okay. As a victim of abuse, I had adopted the response of giving in to others. In my experience, compliance was less painful than fighting. Sadly, this reaction had bled into my daily life, contaminating it as well.

"Sandy, what choices are you making around this situation with your friend?" Margaret asked again, weeks later.

"I guess I'm really choosing not say what I need to say because I'm afraid I will lose this friendship. I realize this is something I do frequently. I put up with a lot or keep problems to myself in order to avoid conflict." I paused for a moment, as I was confronted with my own words; the newly greased wheels were finally turning. I was slowly releasing my belief that I was essentially choice-less. I felt like a caterpillar shedding its protective yet confining shell. Although it was scary at first, the more I flexed my wings, the better I felt.

"You know, Margaret, the truth of the matter is that I have no way of knowing if I will actually lose this friendship if I stand up for myself. And, in actuality, I most likely won't. Based on recent events, I've discovered that people actually seem to respect me rather than turn away from me when I am assertive."

Margaret remained silent while my mind worked this through. "It's time I let go of that fear! It does nothing but hold me back. Besides, now that I see it as a choice, it no longer seems like the big boogie man who won't leave. I can choose to listen and buy in to the lies, or I can choose to believe the truth."

"Yes, yes, Sandy, exactly. You are beginning to see your actions in a new light. You have choices. You're right: you don't have to believe you will lose so much if you are assertive. Knowing this, what other choices could you make?"

I was finally ready to take the plunge, to step out onto that ledge, spread my new fledgling wings, and fly. "Margaret, I have decided that I am ready to set a boundary with my friend. I believe I can do so in love, trusting that I will be okay no matter what the outcome is."

"This is beautiful, Sandy! You are right; you can't predict how your friend will respond, and you are not responsible for how she will handle your choice. But you can trust that you will be okay."

I mentally took Margaret's wise words and translated them for myself. *I can say what I need to say in love and trust God to help my friend handle her own emotions. I do not have to take care of and anticipate her needs in this situation. God will be with her, and likewise, he will be with me. I can trust that God is covering this and will work it out for the good of us both.*

I smiled as I recalled those countless hours on the phone, stretching my mind. It felt as though I was literally rewiring my brain, asking it to think differently than it had for most of my life. It took time to get used to this new paradigm shift, this fundamental change in my approach to life. With God's help and my consistently holding myself accountable for my thoughts, I was finally getting it. My frustration over not being able to help Scott co-lead the group lifted as I saw my situation from the principle of being at choice. I was making an important choice to take care of my body. Scott made a choice to attend the group alone. Though it wasn't what either of us would prefer, we accepted the situation and chose to not let it dampen our spirits. What a peaceful way of looking at our challenge.

My thoughts returned to the day of my perfect storm. Though it has been a difficult journey, many wonderful changes have taken place in my life since that day. What I once perceived as one of the worst days in my life, I now saw as a great blessing. That one devastating event launched me into a journey that would ultimately bring me to this place of peace and freedom. Finally unhooked from my past, I have gone from that victimized, broken girl to a woman, whole and complete, loved by God, whose life, like any other, has meaning, value, and worth. Though I might continue to struggle now and again, I have a treasure trove of wisdom I can recall and apply as needed. Most importantly, these tools have helped me spiritually. Based on scriptural principles, they gave me a newfound faith and trust in God, which brings peace, as he promised, that indeed passes all understanding.

It was in the comfort of these truths that I closed my eyes and drifted off, peacefully awaiting Scott's return.

# SURVIVAL SKILL

# *Live in Choice*

> Everything can be taken from a man but one thing: The last of human freedoms—to choose one's attitude in any given set of circumstances.
>
> Victor Frankel[2]

## SCOTT: THE PERILS OF HAVE-TOS

For years after Sandy's breakdown and the horrible discovery of our sons' traumatizing experiences, my life became driven by a series of have-tos: "I *have to* work extra hours. My family's needs *have to* come before mine. I *have to* disregard certain feelings so I can keep going. My own needs will *have to* wait." Duty and obligation dictated the course of my days to the point that my actions became mechanical. Early on, I developed a "suck it up" mentality just to get through each trying day. Though this state of mind carried me through our times of crisis, it eventually became a liability, leaving me overwhelmed and worn out.

The weight I carried was burdensome. I was running out of steam and quickly sinking into a state of depression.

Making the shift to living my life from a place of choice was agonizing at times and liberating at others. This entire process took time and some creative maneuvering. It didn't happen overnight. There were two main barriers I needed to get past. The first obstacle was my fear that if I let go of my have-to drive I might completely lose all motivation, give up, and succumb to the depression that shadowed me. To overcome this, I cultivated a *want-to* energy to replace the *have-to* push. By choosing to refocus on the benefits of working and what we could gain from the long hours I put in, I no longer felt enslaved to the have-to grind. This shift in attitude actually brought with it the desire to work.

The second hurdle to overcome was that I had always associated choice with something I truly desired and had associated the lack of choice with things I had to do or things that were beyond my reach. This obstacle became a non-issue when I realized that my "choose to" did not always have to line up with my "want to." I realized that I could choose to do something even if I didn't necessarily want to do it. With this adjustment in my approach to life, I no longer felt bullied by my have-tos.

As challenging as it was, this expanded idea of choice changed my life. In fact, it gave me my life back. Unknowingly, I had been lying to myself. In truth, I didn't have to do anything. No one held a gun to my head and said I had to work these long and difficult hours. No one forced me to put my own needs aside and sacrifice for my family. The truth was I was choosing to do these things out of love for them. This realization offered immediate relief. It became evident that my duty-bound depression resulted from the way I mentally framed my situation. It all boiled down to the attitude I chose to take more than what I actually did or didn't do.

With my newfound mindset and the choice to be easy on myself and to take care of myself, I quickly recuperated. As the overwhelming feeling of being trapped subsided, my joy and passion returned. Just realizing the truth that I always had a choice eliminated much of the stress and pressure that my forceful, have-to mentality generated. I'd discovered an invaluable treasure, a key to my freedom from a lifestyle that had imprisoned me for so long.

## SANDY: THE PITFALLS OF CAN'TS

Although I had spent many years learning to temper my people-pleasing behaviors, I often found myself putting my own needs aside in order to ensure the happiness of others. This was, after all, my way of feeling okay about myself. At the time of my breakdown, my obsession with other people's feelings had reached an overwhelming apex. My self-talk was saturated with limiting statements. Phrases such as "I can't say that; what will people think of me?" "I can't do this; I might hurt someone's feelings," "I can't... I can't... I can't" seemed to dominate my thoughts. Although it is good to filter our thoughts in concern for others' feelings, I had taken it to an all-time extreme. My choice-less thinking was so pervasive that I fooled myself into believing that my options must be centered on others, to the exclusion of myself.

It took time and effort to shift my thinking in this area. Due to my nature, I have always placed a high value on my concern for others. However, through my growth process, I've now learned to place the same value on myself, restoring a healthy balance to my thinking and my life.

I've further learned from Jesus's example of service to others. Sacrifice and concern for others is good, but as Christ demonstrated, it is best when it comes from our overflow rather than our reserves. Jesus made a habit of drawing away from everyone to spend time alone with God and recharge his batteries. He also made the ultimate healthy choice: he listened to his Father regarding when to help and when to wait.

As my recovery period neared its end, I was confronted with another set of can'ts. Though I did not share this in our story, once I made the decision to work with women, the Can't Gremlin began pounding at my door. "You can't work with women; who do you think you are, anyway? You're just a former psych patient who couldn't possibly have anything to offer! You can't speak publicly; no one will respect what you have to say." The enemy loves our can'ts and uses them against us well. If we tell ourselves we can't do something, especially something we feel the Lord leading us to do, we've just done our enemy's job for him. Thankfully, I fought through those limiting thoughts. It wasn't easy. I can still find myself battling them, especially when I am in a position where I feel insecure. I tell Scott I often feel like little Nemo, swimming hard to keep up with the big fish. There are some things I can't do alone, but God and I together definitely can.

My situation entailed what we refer to as "perceived can'ts": those things I was capable of doing but convinced myself I couldn't. There are, of course, realistic can'ts. One only has to watch the popular reality television show *American Idol* to see this fact! No amount of positive thinking about being the next American Idol is going to overcome an inability to sing. If you can't carry a tune, you'll never carry the title of the American Idol. To ignore our realistic limitations can be disastrous, or at the very least, as we see at the beginning of each new season of this program, embarrassing!

I discovered this realization the hard way when I ignored the realistic limitations (can'ts) set by the CFS and fibromyalgia. However, I also learned that when I worked within my limitations (respecting my body), I could, at times, do more than I first believed.

## SCOTT AND SANDY

Our decision to live our lives and handle our problems from a place of choice truly changed us and our situation. Once we finally embraced the reality that we always had a choice, we began to experience our lives from a place of freedom. We were then able to move through our struggles with greater ease. Margaret's challenge sent us on a journey of discovery, and her notion that we are at choice was quickly adopted as our fifth and final Survival Skill: *Live in Choice.*

Let us take a moment and explain what we mean by living *in* or *at* choice. Choice, in this context, is much more than merely having a choice or making a decision. It goes beyond the *act* of choosing; it is essentially a *mindset* of choice. Living at choice, therefore, becomes a lifestyle of choice, giving a person a choice-filled approach to life and one's struggles. Actively living at choice means that the decisions we make, the thoughts we think, the words we speak, and actions we take are done from a position of choice. It can positively affect motivations, responses, and actions. Anyone choosing to live at choice will find the shift in their thinking and attitude worth the effort.

---

## IT'S YOUR TURN

### SCOTT AND SANDY

Do choice-less feelings dictate your sense of well-being? Are choice-less thoughts dominating your thinking? Like Scott, perhaps you're feeling burned out by the demands of your oppressive have-tos. Or, like Sandy, maybe you've been held back by your limiting can'ts.

Maybe, overall, you feel choice-less about being able to do anything to change or improve your difficult circumstances. If so, we'd like to challenge that perception and offer you the opportunity to experience the freedom and life-changing transformation that choice can bring into your life, especially during your times of struggle.

## You Always Have a Choice

It may surprise you to discover that you always have a choice, even when choice seems nonexistent. When you tell yourself otherwise, you tell yourself a story. Saying you have no choice simply is not true. Each and every one of us was born with the God-given freedom of choice. From day one, God gave mankind the opportunity to choose. He both desires and expects us to responsibly exercise choice in every area of our lives.

Please note: There are those unique situations where our choices can be stripped from us. Criminal acts, violent crimes, even some natural disasters can be responsible for the theft of one of our most precious freedoms. If you have been an unfortunate victim of this type of loss, our hearts go out to you. We understand the pain you may carry, but there is hope. Though you had no initial control over your circumstance, you can now make choices that will allow you to no longer continue to feel victimized.

Though it may be true that your choices are very limited, you always have a choice regarding your outlook, attitude, and response. This was the case for us. We had no control over what Cat did to us, but we did have a choice as to how we would process it. We could choose to stay victimized and embittered by these actions, or we could choose to take responsibility for how we would handle our situation and what we would do to improve it. Though we were victimized initially, we chose not to continue living as victims. The same can be true for you.

## Moving Beyond Your Circumstances through the Power of Choice

Choice provides you with both the freedom and the power to move beyond your difficult and often seemingly unchangeable circumstances. Let's look at how you can accomplish this practically.

## *Believe That You Have a Choice*

If you are ever to make the appropriate changes and move beyond your difficult situation, you must first believe that you have a choice. If you don't believe that you have a choice to improve or change it, you probably won't. Remember, what you tell yourself is what you will ultimately believe.

When you believe you have no choice over your situation, you will feel victimized by it. You can also become immobilized by limiting can'ts, and you will feel stressed and bullied by have-tos. Like a puppet on a string, you can feel pulled through life, dragged into circumstances over which you believe you have no control.

> If you believe you have no choice, your belief might as well be true, because you will live your life as though you don't.

## *Choose to Live from a Place of Choice*

The reality that you always have a choice doesn't necessarily guarantee that you will actively live your life from a place of choice. You can have the freedom of choice but choose not to exercise it. Consistently living from a position of choice requires a decision and a commitment on your part. When we made this commitment in our own lives, our struggles became more manageable. We felt empowered rather than victimized. This sense of empowerment began to replace an overall feeling of helplessness and hopelessness.

## *Explore Your Options*

Approaching your struggles from a place of choice can help you see options that are available, ones you might never before have considered. Suffering has a way of creating tunnel-vision, which limits our ability to see different alternatives. When we find ourselves caught up in the whirlwind of our problems, our creativity can often be the first thing to go. Without this inspired thinking, we can quickly feel trapped.

Viewing your struggle from a place of choice, on the other hand, can inspire ingenious options. You may well have heard Plato's quote "Necessity is the mother of all invention." When you find yourself being swallowed up by your circumstance, you can stop the cycle by exploring your other options. Below are five steps that can help you identify other options that may be available.

- Take a step back to get some perspective. It is difficult to see your choices when you are caught up in the whirlwind of chaos. Taking an objective look at your situation helps you see other prospects.
- Ask God to help you see the options you might have previously overlooked.
- Get different perspectives from those you trust.
- Don't resist the problem. It is easier to recognize other alternatives when you are not in fight mode. Applying the first survival skill of *acceptance* will aid you in this process.
- Brainstorm and make a list of alternative options, even if you can't see yourself implementing them.

As you explore your options, you may come across choices that you are not quite ready to make. That is okay. That is your choice. Just be aware that choosing not to take action to change your circumstances is actually a choice to keep them the same. When you are ready, you can take the appropriate, forward-moving actions that will positively impact your struggles.

Choosing not to take appropriate, forward-moving action to change your circumstance is making a choice to keep them the same.

## *Eliminate All Choice-less Words and Thoughts*

Take a moment and consider the number of times throughout the course of the day that you think and speak choice-less thoughts and statements: "I have no choice." "You leave me no choice." "I can't." "I have to." If you're like the rest of us, you probably use them more than you realize.

To live in choice is to have a mindset of choice. If you are to maintain a mindset of choice, you will need to eliminate your choice-less thinking. Choice-less thinking leads to defeatist thoughts that will keep you from moving forward.

Watching what you say is equally important because whatever you think internally is reinforced by what you speak externally. Make a commitment to only think and speak choice-full phrases.

Tune in to those times when you are feeling choice-less. Listen to your thoughts and words. Are they choice-less? If so, try a do-over; stop, and start over again, restating your sentence with a "choose to" or "choose not to" statement.

Be patient with yourself during this process. Changing your mental and verbal vocabulary can be tricky, especially when you're just getting started. Be prepared to stutter a little as you catch yourself and search for the proper choice statements. When we began making these changes, our conversations often looked something like this: "I can't (Interruption)... oops, I mean I choose not to." "I have to (Interruption)... no, I mean I choose to." Sometimes we even helped each other make these changes (using wisdom in our timing) by responding with: "Do you mean you're choosing to?" Or, "You mean you're choosing not to?" Or in response to "I don't have a choice," we might respond with, "Remember, we always have a choice." At times we brainstormed together to explore the various choices available. Our only rule in challenging each other was to keep it light and not become critical, condemning, parental, or judgmental.

## Choose to Forgive

As you move through your crisis, you will be faced with the choice to forgive. The choice to forgive those responsible for your pain and suffering can be difficult. The truth is, you may not yet be ready to forgive. However, no matter how difficult, forgiveness is an essential part of the process of moving beyond our struggles.

SCOTT AND SANDY

Forgiveness for both of us was a difficult process, but it was a decision we knew we must make in order to move out from our victimization, follow Christ's example, and be free from Cat. What made forgiveness particularly difficult was that no sooner would we forgive Cat for one offense than we would turn around only to discover another. Whether it was a new action from Cat or a memory uncovered, our rollercoaster ride of forgiveness continued to have its ups and downs. No matter how difficult or frustrating, however, we knew forgiveness was a crucial part of our healing process. With God's help, and after several years of working through it, we were finally able to fully forgive.

Perhaps you're not quite ready to forgive because you first need some time to work through your feelings.

SANDY

This was the case for me. I hadn't understood or uncovered even half of my abuse before my heart wanted to mend the relationship. There is a danger in forgiving too quickly. If one isn't aware of what one is forgiving, it can open the door for further harm from the offending party, or even disappointment and frustration in oneself or the process of forgiveness. When I discovered what happened to our sons, however, I realized I needed more time. I first needed to process through my feelings and wrap my mind around all that had taken place before I was truly ready to forgive.

Maybe you're not ready because you don't fully understand what it means to forgive.

## *Understanding Forgiveness*

Many struggle to forgive simply because they carry misconceptions about what forgiveness truly is. The following are helpful facts to aid you in fully understanding forgiveness:

- Forgiveness is a choice. It is an act of the will. It is not a feeling, nor is it based on feelings. It does not require you to be in a forgiving mood. While it does increase the chance that you will feel forgiving feelings, forgiveness is not dependent on such feelings.

  We chose to forgive Cat as an act of our will, even when it felt as though forgiveness was the last thing we could ever offer that individual. Sometimes it was a daily choice.
- Forgiveness doesn't erase what happened, nor does it imply that the offense is okay. In forgiving, you are not excusing away any injustice or abuse. Forgiveness simply takes vengeance out of your grasp and hands it over to God, trusting him to judge the offending party (Romans 12:19).

  If you are forgiving hurtful or even abusive behaviors that are still taking place, it is important that you set necessary boundaries to stop offending behaviors. This might include anything from limiting your time with this person to obtaining a restraining order or pursuing other legal actions, if necessary.

Allowing God to handle this matter was especially challenging for us. Without taking further legal actions, we were concerned that Cat might believe there were no consequences. We confess that for many years we longed for God to punish Cat. To our great disappointment, it seemed as though Cat was actually prospering instead. It is easy to forgive when you see justice carried out; yet God asks us to forgive even when there is no justice. This was perhaps the most difficult part of our process, but with God's grace, we eventually let go of the need to see Cat's punishment and ultimately forgave this person.

- Forgiving is not the same as forgetting. While forgetting might happen in time, it may not happen at all. Forgetting is not a necessary component of forgiveness. As a matter of fact, sometimes it is important to remember, if it will protect you in the future or help you make a different choice next time.

  For us it was important to remember what had been done. Because Sandy had forgotten what happened to her as a child, she inadvertently exposed our own children to similar abuses.

- Forgiveness is not necessarily deserved. The offending party might not have asked your forgiveness or appear repentant or remorseful. In your opinion, he or she may not deserve it. Forgiveness actually has nothing to do with merit. God instructs us to forgive regardless (Colossians 3:13).

Cat never asked for forgiveness and has never shown repentance or remorse, as far as we know. This person has not done anything to merit our forgiveness. We chose to forgive because God instructs us to and it was necessary for us to move forward, not because we are "super-spiritual" or because Cat deserved it.

- Failure to forgive is harmful. You may have heard the analogy that likens unforgiveness to drinking poison yourself while expecting the other person to die. Failing to forgive will always cause you more damage than those you fail to forgive. Unforgiveness results in resentment, bitterness, and damage to our physical, spiritual, mental, and emotional health. It also impacts our other relationships. It further causes us to continue to feel victimized by those we haven't forgiven. Furthermore, it creates an unhealthy bond to the one who offended us. Unforgiveness also makes us vulnerable to Satan's strategies (2 Corinthians 2:10–11).

  We were well aware of the poison of resentment and bitterness, and that was something we did not want to consume our lives. We worked diligently at the process of forgiveness so as not to give the enemy this foothold.

  We heard an analogy that helped us further: Unforgiveness is like inviting the offending party into your home, into your bed at night, to your breakfast table, into your quiet time with the Lord. By not forgiving, we would become tethered to this person.

- Forgiveness is primarily for you. Forgiveness sets you free and helps you maintain a strong relationship with God. As the quote aptly states, "Forgiveness is setting the prisoner free, only to find out that the prisoner was me" (Lewis B. Smedes[3]).

We can honestly say that for all five of us, forgiveness has brought a true freedom into our lives.

- Forgiveness is not confrontational. The choice to forgive can be granted in the person's presence or outside of it. In other words, the person whom you are forgiving doesn't have to be present in order to be forgiven. If you feel confrontation is necessary but is unsafe or impossible, the alternative of writing a letter that you never intend to send can accomplish the same goal. Such a letter can also be cathartic and healing.

  We chose to forgive Cat without a confrontation.

- Forgiveness is a process. Depending on the depth of pain and loss, it can take time. It's not always a one-time deal. We firmly believe that the degree to which we forgive is dependent upon the degree to which we have processed the pain caused by the offense. As you work through your pain and loss, you might find that you will need to forgive in stages.

  Our forgiveness process took time. Every time one of us went through another layer of healing, we again needed to work through the issue of forgiveness.

- We are instructed to forgive. "And forgive anyone who offends you. Remember, the Lord forgave you, so you must forgive others" (Colossians 3:13 NLT). God gives you everything you need to enable you to forgive. God is not asking you to do something you cannot do.

  How could we ignore something so important to God? Out of love for him and his love for us, we chose to obey, and we're glad we did.

Having gained a correct understanding of what it means to forgive, it is now time to explore the forgiveness process itself. The following steps can help you walk through forgiveness:

- Begin by making a list of those who have offended you, writing out what specifically happened.
- Accept the reality that these things did, in fact, happen. Let go of any whys, if onlys, and shoulds or shouldn'ts that may still be hanging around. At this point, simply accept what happened without trying to figure it out.
- Acknowledge the pain and hurt you experienced; don't minimize or overdramatize it. Journaling your feelings may be a great asset at this time. Allow yourself to feel your feelings as fully as needed. Remember, you will experience the benefits of forgiveness to the degree that you process through the pain and wounding those events caused.
- Transfer the person and the offense over to God. You might find it helpful to visualize yourself taking the offense to God. Some see themselves burying the wrongdoing at the foot the cross; others imagine placing the offense in a box and either handing it to God or tying it to a balloon and allowing it to float to him. There are several ways to picture this; you can find what best fits your needs.
- Set any boundaries that may need to be set. Good, healthy limits can lessen the opportunity for further offenses.
- Reframe your situation by looking for the good that has, or will, come from your painful experience.
- Eliminate any stories you may be telling yourself about your experience that may be magnifying your pain.
- Take responsibility for your role, if any, in the situation.
- Make the choice to forgive.

- Stop revisiting the experience, both in your own mind and in rehashing it with others. Processing the offense with the goal of bringing closure is one thing, but rehashing it will only serve to keep your hurts alive.
- Forgive yourself. Sometimes the hardest one to forgive is you. Forgiveness is a choice. Though it may be difficult, you can choose to forgive yourself.

After you have forgiven, it may be necessary to set further boundaries. Boundaries are invisible, flexible, yet firm borders we establish to keep us emotionally and/or physically safe. When we forgave Cat, we set a boundary to keep this individual out of our lives. We initially started with a restraining order. Later, our boundary was simply based on the decision to have no further contact. Due to the toxicity of this relationship, though we continue to pray for Cat, we maintain these boundaries. Many people confuse healthy boundaries with the use of anger, bitterness, and resentment as a way of self-protection. These harmful, negative emotions are not necessary when you assertively implement firm, healthy boundaries in their place.

## CONCLUSION: STILL GETTING THIS THING CALLED CHOICE

The survival skill of choice is actually foundational to all other survival skills. The rest are possible because of the free gift of choice. As we have already mentioned, the choice to change is yours to make. Just remember, the choice to do nothing is a choice to remain the same.

We are still getting this thing called choice. We slip up from time to time. But it's okay. With time and practice we will all improve in living at choice. Exercising the power of choice in your life will open up a whole new world for you as it did for us. Take it slow. Fully living in choice is a process and takes time.

You may be replacing a lifetime of choice-less thinking and acting, but we know you can make this change if you choose to.

You now have at your disposal the five Survival Skills (Acceptance, Good, Truth, Choice, and Personal Responsibility) that God used to change our lives and help us move past our pain and devastation. With God's empowerment, these skills can help you make it through whatever life brings your way. But please don't just settle for survival. Determine to grow and flourish as you move beyond just surviving. We want to leave you with the challenge to take these life-saving principles and turn them into permanent life skills. With these skills in hand, you have the potential to live a life of fulfillment, peace, joy, and contentment, regardless of your circumstances. Our prayers are with you as you endeavor to live beyond survival.

# *Closure*

SANDY

"Hello, Sandy."

"Hi, John, what's up?"

"Stacie and I thought you'd want to know that Jack has been ill for some time and is now dying. If you wanted to see him one last time before he goes, you should consider doing it soon. We'd be happy to go with you and Scott; just let us know."

My breath caught in my throat as I heard the devastating news. "Thank you for sharing this news, John. I'll call you back soon," I concluded as I eased the phone back into the cradle.

Jack was a dearly loved, elderly family member of mine whom we hadn't seen for many years due to the distance we'd put between ourselves and the family. Unsure as to whom we could trust, we took no chances and pulled away from everyone until we could sort things out. We had been through too much to allow any further destruction. After a brief conversation, Scott and I decided our family was in a strong enough place now to take a calculated risk. We would go, but our sons would remain safely at home.

Though I was determined to live my life without being stifled by my fear of encountering Cat, knowing that a real opportunity to express my empowerment was impending, anxiety began to set in. In spite of the giant butterflies that threatened my stomach, I called John back and set up a visit for that evening.

Our time together, though painful, went surprisingly well. Thankfully, Cat was not in attendance. Anita, Jack's wife, was grateful we had come and held on tightly as we embraced. The living room had been rearranged to allow for Jack's hospital bed. Jack was barely with us and death seemed to overshadow the entire room. Scott and I approached the bed with John and Stacie beside us while several cousins waited patiently for us to have our moment of grief. As I gazed over the wasting frame of this once strong and robust man, my heart ached at the realization of all we had missed these many years we were putting our lives back together. Time was gone, and I could not get it back. In acceptance, I leaned in to whisper my final good-byes. As we eased away from the bed, we were engulfed in a solemn welcome we had not expected from several cousins. Though we were still a bit wary, it felt good to be with my family once again.

The ride home with John and Stacie was filled with talk of memories of Jack. As the conversation shifted to the impending funeral, Scott and I shared our concern about a possible confrontation with Cat. We wanted to avoid a public scene, so the four of us discussed all possible scenarios and made appropriate plans. If we were stepping into precarious territory, we weren't doing so without solid preparation.

The day of the funeral arrived, and all was going according to plan. Thankfully, the funeral home had respected our request to reserve the back row, as the service was well attended. With the closing prayer we quickly and quietly got up to make our way out ahead of the crowd. To our surprise, several members of the family saw us leaving and silently rushed to catch us. Soon we were making plans to meet at the nearest restaurant to catch up.

We began to allow ourselves the luxury to relax and enjoy this little reunion when we realized the need to stick with our plan to leave before we ran into Cat. Saying good-bye to the last person, we turned to take the walkway into the parking lot. As we rounded the corner we found ourselves facing down the very person we'd hoped to avoid. Cat was blocking our only way out.

Fear threatened to freeze me in my tracks, but I refused to give in. A healthy respect for danger is one thing, but a paralyzing fear is something I did not want dictating my life. I was ready for this. I would not allow a repeat of the hospital scene. *God did not give me a spirit of fear, but one of power, love, and a sound mind,* I encouraged myself as I quoted 2 Timothy 1:7. *I can do this! I have the inner strength and resolve, God's love can conquer anything, and this time I do possess a sound mind.*

It wasn't that I despised or hated this person; on the contrary, in spite of all that had been done, I had spent many years working out my forgiveness of Cat. I was concerned, however, about what kind of affect this person might have on my family and me if we were in close proximity. After all, the spiritual battle God eventually freed us of was deeply connected with this individual. I did not want to invite anything remotely resembling that sort of thing into our lives again. Yet, here I was, face-to-face, with the person who had catapulted the lives of my family into chaos and anguish.

Stepping forward, I took a deep breath to steady myself, squeezed Scott's hand for support, and offered a quick prayer for protection and discernment. Cat wasn't easy to read; what you thought might be true often wasn't the case. But I wasn't here to figure out Cat. I wanted to prove to both Cat and myself that I was no longer afraid. This simple step was a testament to all that I had overcome and to the healing, growth, and empowerment I received through God's work in my life.

Silence loomed like a heavy fog as we stood facing each other, neither knowing what to say. What happened next I've decided to take at face value, as I am uncertain as to Cat's true intentions. Reaching out, Cat took me in an embrace and began to cry. "I love you," Cat whispered through the tears. In the past, this type of affection was often manipulative, intended to illicit a conforming and submissive response. Being softhearted, this was typically all it would take for me to cave and go on as if all were right and okay between us, regardless of what had been done. Over these last several years, my heart, thankfully, had not hardened, but it had gained in wisdom and discernment. I had learned the importance of healthy and firm boundaries, even with family members. Therefore, I did not experience the typical compulsion to give in. Dry eyed, without coercion, and in full possession of my faculties, I genuinely responded, "I love you too." My statement was not an intimation of a desire to reconnect but rather, my way of releasing this person. The encounter lasted but a moment, yet in that short span of time we came to an unspoken understanding: There would be no admission of guilt; there would be no repentance. We would live our lives respecting an invisible boundary drawn through the city. Yet one thing was clear: there was forgiveness. And with that, we each went our own separate ways.

SCOTT

Since the discovery of Cat's attacks against my family and me, I often wondered how I would react if and when our paths ever crossed. Would I feel hatred and anger? Would I feel compelled to assault this person? Would I yell at the top of my lungs, "Cat's a predator! Protect your kids"? Would I demand that this person take responsibility for what was done, repent, and beg my forgiveness? At one time I might have. But oddly enough, I felt no anger, no bitterness. There was no desire for vengeance, no demand for an explanation or even an apology. It wasn't as if everything was all right, it just was. I felt neutral, non-reactive, and strangely okay.

As we drove home that evening following a pleasant dinner with several of Sandy's family, I reflected on how impressed I was with our responses to Cat. With God's grace and empowerment and a good amount of hard work on our part, we both had truly changed.

# *Epilogue: Beyond Survival*

SCOTT AND SANDY

Our lives today are a far cry from what they were. For this, we are extremely grateful. We enjoy a freedom and fullness of life that no matter what our circumstances, we know God is at work in our lives and we can trust him to bring about good in it. Life is no longer heavy and dark. Like a smooth, shiny pebble on the beach, tumbled, shaped, and polished by the storm we weathered, our lives have been transformed.

Scott was gradually able to let go of his vigilant, protective stance and overcame his "burn out" state as well. He made this shift by placing the ultimate covering and protection of his family in God's hands. He further discovered that through choices to manage his schedule, take better care of himself, and by replacing his have-tos with choose-tos, his life overall feels less stressful and more enjoyable.

Sandy is now a certified life coach and has discovered healthy ways to manage the CFS and fibromyalgia by honoring her body, mind, and spirit. Having worked through her past abuse, she is no longer haunted by traumatic memories. She works daily to keep her thoughts and emotions in check and has exchanged her paralyzing fear of Cat for healthy boundaries. Her attitude and outlook on life stem from a deep conviction that God is in control and indeed works every detail in the lives of those who love him into something good (Romans 8:26–28 MSG).

Together, we are doing well. As a result of our commitment to each other, our marriage is stronger than ever. We both feel loved, appreciated, and valued within our relationship. Even our teamwork has been strengthened by our experiences.

Our little boys are now grown men. Throughout the years they have periodically struggled with the effects of their trauma. Yet with each go-around they have come through as stronger, healthier individuals. They too have worked hard on their recovery and have refused to allow their past to derail their future. Each one walks intimately with the Lord and is succeeding in his field of choice. Needless to say, we are proud of the tremendous faith, hard work, and teachable attitudes each of our sons has shown through the course of their difficult journey. We are honored to be the parents of such brave, wise, and godly men.

• • •

Throughout our journey there were times when we honestly couldn't see how things would work out. In our darkest moments, we often lost sight of all hope. Thankfully, our God is a God of hope and never leaves us, especially in those dark hours. Though we might have felt alone, we never truly were. God was working, even then, to draw us closer to him and bring about greater growth in our lives.

By introducing us to these five skills, God showed us a way to move beyond our painful circumstances. The decision was ours as to what we would do with these principles. We are not super saints; we merely made a choice not to allow our experiences to dictate our lives and hold us back from all God had for us. Instead, we were determined to move forward and were dedicated to doing whatever was required to make that happen. These same opportunities are available to you; all that is required is that you are willing to put forth the effort.

Outside of Christ's, no life is perfect, and ours is no exception. Like you, we continue to experience life in its full range of ups and downs. Life isn't always easy, but it is good. Our choices and attitudes can make it better or make it worse. We look forward to the future with confidence and assurance. We daily choose, with God's help, to *accept what is, look for the good, tell ourselves the truth, live in choice,* and *take responsibility* for our decisions and actions. In so doing, we are experiencing the fullness of life God offers. And it is good!

Your circumstances will change you. Why not allow them to change you for the better?

When you face each day and every situation with these five skills and have God at the helm, you too can rise above any problem. Remember, God's love and blessings are available for all his children. For those who don't yet hold this title, know that he loves you and sacrificed everything to give you the opportunity to choose this wonderful adoption. Never forget that you are extremely special and very deeply loved.

# REFERENCES

Backus, William D., Chapian, Marie, *Telling Yourself the Truth,* 1980, Bethany House Publishers.

Bill Purvis Ministries, Cascade Hills Church, Columbus, GA, http://www.billpurvis.com March, 2010.

Kottler, Jeffrey A., Brown, Robert W., *Introduction to Therapeutic Counseling,* 1985, Wadsworth, Inc.

Ruth Hadikin BSc RM RN Cert.Ed CC, Life Coach whose dialogue was paraphrased. Though not cited in our book, Ruth is also the author of *Effective Coaching in Healthcare,* 2004, Edinburgh London, Elsevier Science Limited.

Tom Stone, Great Life Technologies: Core Dynamics of Common Problems

# ENDNOTES

1 J. W. Chapman, The Life and Work of D.L. Moody, 1900

2 Kottler, Jeffrey A., Brown, Robert W., *Introduction to Therapeutic Counseling,* 1985, Belmont, CA 94002, Wadsworth, Inc. page 89.

3 Lewis B. Smedes, "Forgiveness - The Power to Change the Past," *Christianity Today,* 7 January 1983